MANDELA

MANDELA

HIS LIFE AND LEGACY
FOR SOUTH AFRICA
AND THE WORLD

By Bob Crew

Skyhorse Publishing

Skyhorse Publishing books may be purchased in bulk at special discounts for sales promotion, corporate gifts, fund-raising, or educational purposes. Special editions can also be created to specifications. For details, contact the Special Sales Department, Skyhorse Publishing, 307 West 36th Street, 11th Floor, New York, NY 10018 or info@skyhorsepublishing.com.

Skyhorse® and Skyhorse Publishing® are registered trademarks of Skyhorse Publishing, Inc.®, a Delaware corporation.

Visit our website at www.skyhorsepublishing.com.

10 9 8 7 6 5 4 3 2 1

Library of Congress Cataloging-in-Publication Data is available on file.

ISBN: 978-1-62914-337-8

Printed in the United States of America

Acknowledgments

B ECAUSE THE VAST majority of the black, white, and brown South Africans to whom I have spoken, or whom I have interviewed off-record in order to write this book, have not wanted to reveal their identities for obvious reasons of personal security in their racially divided country—or because they have other things to lose by talking openly to me about matters of a politically or racially sensitive nature—I cannot, alas, acknowledge them by name.

But they all know who they are and will recognize themselves as and when they are anonymously quoted or written about in these pages, and they will know how grateful I am to them for having taken the time to speak to me in the different South African towns and cities in which we have met.

They are people of all races, up and down the social ladder, at all levels of employment—museum staff, craftsmen, restaurateurs, waiters and other retail service workers, taxi drivers and tradesmen, schoolteachers, slum dwellers, financial, professional, and business people, and in some cases their families as well, several of whom have invited me into their homes. In particular there is a jokey and smiling young black teenager in Soweto who took me in and out of the homes of shantytown dwellers and sent his best personal regards to the Queen of England! There are many such teenagers working in this way in Soweto, so I am not giving too much away about him here, and what he has had to say does not put him at much risk, but others have taken a big risk talking to me as they have, as will be seen in the pages of this book, and they have all provided me with some seriously interesting extracurricular genre pictures and images of life at the grass roots in South Africa that I have been happy to include for extra color, as well as for an important extra dimension of understanding of what ordinary people are thinking and saying about their political leaders and racial others in this suitably discursive book. The genre pictures that these people provide—editorial sketches and scenes of a certain type in the very different situations in which I have found them—really are a big eye-opener to what is going on in the lives and minds of ordinary South African people to whom Nelson Mandela and Jacob Zuma have related in one way or another for better or worse. Their images are intriguing and atmospheric because of the background insights and glimpses that they provide into what people are thinking and how they are behaving in their respective backwaters and byways, and these images are very likely chief among the things that differentiate this book from others.

Because these byway people have relevant and useful things to say, they deserve to be heard (Nelson Mandela quite often took the time to talk to such people in order to find out what they were thinking and how). They are all generally interesting and have a place therefore in this general-interest book about Nelson Mandela and President Zuma (as well as about South Africa and its recent history) and how these two presidents have run South Africa, each in their own different ways, and the big difference that this can make to the future of South Africa today.

I acknowledge and thank all who have spoken to me and given me their time.

Contents

Preface

THE SAD DEATH this month of the former founding-president of South Africa, Nelson Mandela, is the reason for this book that commemorates a truly great political leader who almost certainly made the world a better place—better racially, morally, and politically (a far from perfect world, but certainly a better world in consequence).

I last heard from the late Nelson Mandela—via his office—in 2004 in response to a poem that I wrote about him and his life when he sent me his Christmas greetings, and now that he has died, this book is my final greetings to him, posthumously, by return. I have been regularly traveling far and wide in South Africa for the last decade, talking to and interviewing people for a book about a country that I know well and whose people are certainly well liked by me and so many other British and foreign visitors, as well as by most of the media observers and analysts who go there (I am a former *Times* and *Financial Times* correspondent in London). Whilst, as we shall see in these pages, there are still white, black, and brown racists not to like in South Africa today, there are plenty of white and other non-racists who are very likable, and it has been my pleasure to have met so many of them.

When the black South African author and master storyteller, Chinua Achebe, observed that "until lions learn to produce their own historians, the history of the hunt will continue to glorify the hunter," perhaps he had Nelson Mandela in mind as one of the lions. Here was a lion of a hunted man who certainly knew how to produce and write his own history in his lifetime. When, back in the late 1980s and early 1990s, the apartheid authorities finally realized that they would sooner or later have to bow to global economic sanctions and diplomatic pressures to release Nelson Mandela and his African National Congress (ANC) colleagues—to release Mandela from Pollsmoor Prison in Cape Town and Robben Island before that—after keeping him locked up for twenty-seven years, they hatched a cunning plan. This was at a time when, as Nelson Mandela has told us in his autobiography, the black "townships were on the brink of open warfare," while life went on as before for whites, "placidly" and also "undisturbed."

The apartheid authorities' cunning plan was that some of Mandela's white prison wardens and others should start being nice to him for a change! Before his final release they took him on outings beyond the prison gates—after he went through "fifteen locked metal doors" to get there—and they also got one of the younger white wardens to invite Mandela to his home and introduce him to his wife and children in order to demonstrate a human touch. Talk about too little too late!

But, as Mandela made perfectly clear in his autobiography *Long Walk to Freedom*, he "well knew" that these slippery authorities had a secret "motive" to get him "so used to the pleasures of small freedoms" that he "might be willing," when the time came for his release, "to compromise" in order to have his "complete freedom," while the political deal of what was to be done with the whites when the ANC came to power after 1990 might also be compromised. This was exactly the hypocritical and shameful behavior that was to be expected from the apartheid whites, not only those who worked in the prison where Mandela was held, but in white society at large. But the old fox Mandela was not, of course, taken in by any of this, not having been born yesterday, so the other prisoners and their prison wardens clearly had not read his character very well (as we shall do in this book), as they pathetically and not very cleverly clutched at straws in this way.

As much as Mandela has said that he enjoyed it when some of his prison wardens were suddenly being nice to him for a change, he knew that they had been put up to it by the authorities and he would of course have known that they would not have been being genuinely nice to him otherwise, even if they had wanted to, which was a very big if! Why would they have wanted to, since they had volunteered to serve the apartheid cause and give him and his black ANC colleagues a hard time when they joined this white racist prison service, before the authorities back then realized that they could no longer get away with this? Wicked world indeed! When Nelson Mandela and others in the ANC first found themselves behind bars on Robben Island, they suffered verbal and physical abuse at the hands of their bullying Afrikaner wardens, and Nelson was only allowed one visit and one letter every six months!

But Nelson Mandela went along with this let's-be-nice-to-him charade as the time for his release approached, and he was no doubt much amused and intrigued by it. He was even gracious enough to put one of the wardens ("a very pleasant young man") and his wife and children on his Christmas card list; this shows the good Christian and public relations man that Mandela was, believing in the power of redemption, forgiveness, and racial reconciliation, and setting the famous

Mandela example for others to follow, doing his best to save the wicked whites from themselves.

But the fact that two or three prison wardens were told to start behaving completely out of character to Mandela—faking their friendliness—hardly made them his friends, because they had certainly not been his friends and they certainly did not know him. If they claimed to have been his friends and to have known him after his release from jail—as I have heard it said that they did and that there is even a commercially opportune book being published about this now that he is dead—then their claims were of course taken with a large pinch of salt by those who knew better. Their contact with him was "friendly" only because they had been ordered to be friendly, and it was at a time that Nelson Mandela described that he was "talking with the enemy," not with his friends. However friendly they may have seemed, they were still the enemy until Mandela's release in 1990 when apartheid began to be dismantled and the groundwork was laid principally by blacks for a democratic and non-racist South Africa for the first time in its history.

One of the objects of this book is to get the recent and present history right (it is still in danger of coming out wrong!) at a time when, in Mandela's absence, all sorts of people will no doubt come forward with claims of having been his friend— some two decades later (what kept them so long?)—now that he is no longer around to contradict them, people who did not know his story and have not read his autobiography. We can also expect his old enemies to come forward and tell us all how overrated or useless he was or what a crook Zuma is, or how much they rated or respected Mandela when they did no such thing.

But this is not just a book about Nelson Mandela. It is also about Jacob Zuma, the current president of South Africa, in whose hands we find the precious Mandela legacy from here on, so there is as much if not more about Zuma in these pages as there is about Mandela, with the editorial content divided between the two, as well as relevant others in passing who are all part of the Mandela story. This is a general-interest book about them all and about South Africa under Mandela, and about Zuma now that Mandela has gone.

My guiding principle in writing this book—as in any other books of historical or political biography for that matter—is to seek truth in the unexpected detail of the lives of the late Nelson Mandela and President Zuma, rather than telling people what they and the world already know about them because they have read or heard it already in the media. To this end there are unexpected details, new ideas, and in-depth observations in these pages about the respective character developments and psychologies of Nelson Mandela and President Zuma: about their being Shakespeare fans; about their leadership and character differences; and also about the kind of amazing icon that Nelson Mandela became and why, comparing him with the other great political and historical icons of British and Indian history (since the Brits and the Indians have been the chief players in South Africa, along with the shameful Dutch-Afrikaners—the Indians since Mahatma Gandhi in the late nineteenth and early twentieth centuries prior to 1947 when the Afrikaners took over after the British left).

This is the nature of the biography that is offered in these pages and, in these respects, this book is unlike any other, because this has not been done before with regard to both

Nelson Mandela and President Zuma. So this really is a groundbreaking book.

When people die, it is only natural that we discuss them and what they will and will not be missed and remembered for and what we did and did not like about them—this happens because that's what human beings are like and what many if not most of them do before they move on and forget—and if the dead are great people who wielded power, it stands to reason that they are the ones who get discussed more than others. But it is how they get discussed that matters and whether it is prejudiced and partisan or not, whether it excludes or includes all the credit due, covers all the angles, disputes the right or the wrong things (or puts in the poison one last time!), and also whether the discussions bring anything new to the table, as is my intention in this book.

As many will know and others will not (or can usefully be reminded), this is the challenge and the task for all writers of biographical history, so writers need to do their best to get their research right. But let me say very clearly in this preface that I have not attempted to cover all the well-trodden ground about Nelson Mandela, and this is because it has been well covered already in his own excellent autobiography, as well as in other books, and not least in the late Anthony Sampson's official biography of Nelson Mandela. Sampson was the pioneering editor of *Drum* magazine in South Africa where he went to work and live after being brought up in Hampstead in North London and getting his degree at Oxford University in English literature. He was a writer who worked the magic of losing his whiteness when writing about black South Africa. With his *Anatomy of Britain* and *New Europeans* books, Sampson was, for sure, king of the road! But his Mandela book is certainly and inevitably dated these days. The ability of a white author to lose his or her whiteness when writing about other races in this world really is to be prized, if we are ever to transcend and be at home with the differences of our racial opposites in a much-needed common purpose. This either comes naturally to people, or it does not (I believe that it has always come naturally to me, probably because I have never had any fear of racial or colored others whom I have seen, for better or worse, as fellow human beings and racial equals, with the same hearts and minds as my own). In my opinion, this doesn't mean that a white author becomes another race. It simply means that much or most of the time he or she doesn't let his or her whiteness blind or get in the way, and does not fear the racial difference in question.

What I have attempted to cover in this book for popular interest are only the salient and celebratory facts, in addition to all the unexpected lesser-known details, of the lives of Nelson Mandela and Jacob Zuma—while at the same time taking the recent and present-day temperature and mood of South Africa and where it is likely to go from here—telling this in a very human-interest way, moving the story on since the Sampson biography and the Mandela autobiography.

The popular and human interest approach that I have adopted in these pages seems to have worked well with the likes of the well-known black African author and journalist Jideofor Adibe, PhD, LLM, who emails me to say that he has read my book with "relish" and regards it as "important," so hopefully this is a work that will also appeal to like-minded others. It has certainly appealed to the publisher Guy Sewell at the eminently respected and rigorously intelligent Anglo-American radical cum intellectual publishing company, Verso

Books in London and New York, who has emailed me to say that he has found the time to read my book "with interest" and how "very interesting" and "thought-provoking" it is. With an emphasis on political and social theory, economics, and philosophy, I guess that Verso—publishing the likes of Noam Chomsky, Edward Said, and the 1992 Nobel Prize–winning Rigoberta Menchú, among so may distinguished others—knows a thing or two about these matters and has relevant things to say about them to the likes of classic Liberals like me and no doubt a goodly number of United States Democrats as well.

Whether biographies are more reliable and truthful than autobiographies is a hard question to answer, given that some great people are not capable of writing about themselves frankly and truthfully or without bias (in my opinion, Nelson Mandela certainly was capable). In my experience there is such a thing as an instinctive "ring of truth" that comes across in the way in which books or newspaper articles are reasoned and in the words that are chosen in order to express them. Even so, some authors are better with words than others and can tell more or less of the truth that confronts them, and whatever their truths, it is always only their own interpretation, which may or may not be all of the truth, which is why we need several different versions in order to get at the truth, the whole truth, and nothing but the truth, all of which cannot be told in a single book. But truthful or not, at least autobiographies allow us into the heads and hearts of their authors, if that is where we are interested to go in order to draw our own conclusions about them and the subjects they address.

People who are not capable or do not have the time to write their autobiographies often employ the services of ghostwriters who put words into their mouths for them (and maybe ideas into their heads), when it is anybody's guess who is telling the story!

I once read and helped to promote in London the autobiography of the late Boris Yeltsin in 1990—Russia's first democratically elected president in the post-Soviet era whom I met, interviewed, and partied with in London—which was a very wooden and boring read! However, it was a historically useful and apparently honest book for all that. But, without doubt, the autobiographies and biographies that are a pleasure to read—on account of their writing style—are the ones that are probably better remembered for the literary or intellectual pleasure they have given in addition to the subject matter. We all tend to favor and better remember—don't we?—whatever it was that gave us pleasure, rather than the mediocre stuff that did not, the latter of which is therefore best forgotten (unless the pleasure that it did not give us was so shocking that we cannot forget it, however much we may wish to do so!).

Biographies have been written and published since the time of the ancient Greeks and Romans whilst autobiographies have been written and published in Britain since the nineteenth century (before that since the Middle Ages). Many of these old autobiographies have been narrowly personal and even domesticated and not broadly historical. But today, biographical and autobiographical histories have become much broader in scope, and they are now one of the fastest-growing areas of English-language publishing; and there is, gladly, an increasing African and Asian presence that is emerging in these English-language books.

As almost everybody knows, the Mandela legacy is one of freedom, democracy, moral conscience, racial reconciliation, forgiveness, and equality for all in a racially divided country that is fueled by a capitalist economy with an orderly, law-abiding, and hopefully socially responsible and acceptable financial face; the latter of which is proving increasingly difficult these days, not just in South Africa, but worldwide, and not least for South Africa's desperately poor and needy whose dire poverty has not yet been relieved. But there is no widespread personal criticism that one can see of the late Nelson Mandela for this, only of his office and the ANC administrations that followed him when he retired from politics in 1999.

Whilst some of his critics say that he pandered too much to South Africa's whites and that he spent too much time on glamorous foreign relations abroad, enjoying his celebrity status there—instead of spending more time on job creation and crime prevention at home—it is hard to see what else he could have done in the circumstances in order to attract much-needed foreign investment to an economically declining South Africa that he inherited from the white apartheid regime that went before him. He was also busy preventing a bloody civil war in South Africa by paying close attention to interracial peacekeeping at home (see the introduction that follows this preface), which meant regularly engaging with white and other racial and political factions rather than estranging them. It is not to be underestimated what a precarious knife-edge the country was on where likely revolution and civil war was concerned. And if anyone is at fault for not solving the problems of job creation and crime at home, perhaps it was Nelson Mandela's deputy at that time, Thabo Mbeki, who was presumably supposed to be solving these problems while Mandela was away (Mandela was reportedly critical of Mbeki). Certainly, Mbeki was well qualified with his economics degrees to address these problems, which is why he eventually succeeded Mandela as president, but should Mandela have kept a closer eye on him and taken more responsibility for his lack of progress in such challenging and urgent matters affecting millions of South Africa's desperately poor people?

Perhaps the apparently impossible problems of job creation for millions, as well as poverty and crime at home, were the inevitable price to be paid for the otherwise brilliant success of the Mandela years, unless it was the price to be paid for his office and his ANC colleagues letting him down in these respects while he was busy keeping the peace and globe-trotting in order to attract foreign investments into South Africa (from the multinationals and others) and to keep them there. For sure, Mandela was an amazing public relations man for a nation with a terribly racist public image that was much in need of vastly improved PR, race relations, and foreign relations on so many different fronts. Mandela had to prove to the outside world that, without its whites in government, the ANC had the intelligence and abilities to govern, at least as well as the whites who had governed previously, and he certainly proved this in no uncertain manner. He had to prove that he and his untested ANC government ministers were credible and capable. With common consent, Nelson Mandela was the fatherly moral conscience of South Africa, a truly herculean figure who was and no doubt will continue to be a hard act to follow. He was, uniquely, the liberation hero who had put away his gun (he had to dig a hole and hide it in his garden when the apartheid police came to arrest him!) and also the wise peacemaker who became the heart and soul of his nation.

He really was a man for all seasons with many parts to play in his lifetime—freedom fighter (not from choice, but he rose to the occasion), wise and forgiving interracial negotiator, long-suffering prisoner (a staggering twenty-seven years and more), outstanding politician and democratically elected president, educated (the first in his family) and professional lawyer (by his own admission he was born to be a tribal herdboy), talented author, saintly icon, and thoroughly decent human being! He was never a terrorist who terrorized the apartheid whites who terrorized him and his people and turned him into a freedom fighter by their brutally racist actions (nine out of ten of whom did not even know or care that he was an educated man or law-abiding lawyer, whites to whom, as he said, he did not object as whites, but for their oppression rather).

In recent months Nelson Mandela has been dancing with death—going in and out of the hospital, suffering and also surviving (with the aid of life support) his recurring lung infection and the pneumonia that refused to go away—until, finally, death got him in the end, in his ninety-fifth year, as in the end it gets us all, of course. His demise left millions of his black and white fans in South Africa and across the world grieving and mourning for one of the greatest political leaders of all time—certainly the greatest in South Africa and Africa.

During his remaining days in the hospital—when he was clearly at death's door with no prospect of recovery and unable to speak—he unified South Africa without uttering a word, as nationwide vigils and prayer services were held for him, and the pulse rate of Christian prayer across his country was good and strong when his long-lingering demise doubtless became the most widely and consistently reported in political and racial history anywhere in the world!

Many South African blacks have related to Nelson Mandela at a personal level, not simply politically, as we have seen from how they have consistently prayed for his recovery, just as they would for a member of their own family. To them he was a living saint so sensitively close to their hearts and so affectionately kept in their minds, and for this reason it has been widely reported that there has been a "dark and gloomy cloud" hanging over South Africa as the great man's recurring ill health has refused to go away.

But now that the cloud has finally dispersed, let the cleansing and healing rains come to wash away the grief; let the dancing and the celebrating begin (it already has on the streets of South Africa).

The quasi-religious devotion and mysticism that Nelson Mandela inspired among his followers for all sorts of cultural, racial, and psychological reasons (in addition to the usual reasons of our not wanting to lose loved ones) are not difficult to understand in view of the agonizing history that he and his followers endured. He has been their great savior and liberator—end of story—and has also liberated their former white persecutors from themselves.

The extraordinary, worshipful hold that he has had on his people has been similar to that of the Pope on the Catholic faithful, and not least because, of course, the blacks who revere Mandela would not be where they are today without him. But, although his people, like all good disciples, have been reluctant to let him go and to let death take its natural course, their hopes of keeping him alive became increasingly false during his final months and weeks, as he lingered on, slowly but surely running out of his life's breath, until, at last, he has finally gone.

When this year's news of Nelson Mandela's death in Johannesburg in his ninety-fifth year suddenly reached

London—on the evening of December 5th on the fateful day of his death—purely by chance his *Long Walk to Freedom* biopic film was being shown at the first night of the 2013 Royal Performance premier at the Odeon cinema in Leicester Square in London's West End.

Nelson's daughter Zindzi was in the audience among British and American showbiz and other celebrities and VIPs—including the Duke and Duchess of Cambridge, Prince William, and Kate Middleton—and after the film had been shown, the audience was told of Nelson Mandela's death!

One can imagine the predictable gasps, murmurs, and stunned silence among people who thought they had turned out to watch a celebratory film about the dying man, not an announcement of his actual death.

How ironic and extraordinary was that?

Such an extraordinary and dramatic coincidence indeed.

Was this art imitating life or life imitating art?

For the death of such a monumental world leader to be announced on stage in a cinema and so dramatically in this theatrical way—informing the high-society audience that Mandela had finally departed the world political stage—was a fitting reminder that Mandela had indeed lived his life so dramatically and spectacularly on the world stage. He had departed his life's long and epic walk to freedom at the same time as people were watching a film about it and while he had walked off the world stage to a shorter walk to freedom of a very different kind!

It was as if his ghost had swiftly popped into the Odeon cinema to take a final bow before bowing out, never to return!

When his daughter Zindzi learned of her extraordinary father's death in this highly extraordinary way, she took to the stage with the film's New York producer, Harvey Weinstein, to hold a formal moment of silence, after which a glum-faced Prince William paid an impromptu Mandela tribute for the television news cameras outside the cinema.

And now, as this book goes to press, one of the biggest state funerals of recent times is being organized in South Africa, for which millions are expected to turn out on the streets, while millions more watch it worldwide on television. It is against this immediate background that this book has been published—so here's to Nelson Mandela, South Africa's favorite son and former father of his nation and grandfather of his nation's children, he who will be remembered with the greatest affection, and here's to President Zuma as well, who must now keep the Mandela legacy.

Bob Crew, BA (Hons), MA
Hampstead Garden Suburb
North London
England
December 2013

Introduction

WHEN SEVENTY-TWO THOUSAND people packed into the Wembley soccer stadium in North West London to mark the occasion of Nelson Mandela's seventieth birthday and sang "Free Nelson Mandela" in 1988— watched by six hundred million television viewers in some sixty-seven countries worldwide—the racist white apartheid regime in South Africa finally got it into its thick skull that the time was long overdue for it to do the moral thing and correct the error of its wicked ways by releasing Nelson Mandela from his life sentence behind bars, for which he had already served twenty-seven years.

While it wasn't only, of course, the "Free Nelson Mandela" pop festival and song that got him released from jail—it was economic sanctions and political representations at the highest level—this festival and song certainly attracted global attention to Nelson Mandela as a force for moral good in the world. He was born as a global celebrity in London's Wembley Stadium in this way, as was the power of pop music as a means of moral and political protest, and there had been nothing like it previously either in a national soccer stadium or at a globally televised pop festival with such an earth-shattering political protest, reportedly for six hundred million TV viewers.

Having been born seventy years earlier, the black anti-apartheid campaigner and freedom fighter, Nelson Mandela, was born again in 1988, and it seems fitting to remember this now that he has sadly died this month, because it was this festival that launched him on his way and globalized his cause—that implanted a global image of him and his essential goodness in the minds of millions around the world.

The festival was the brainchild of the English pop music impresario and producer Tony Hollingsworth, and it was given eleven hours of air time by BBC Television's Alan Yentob (hats off to them both), the latter being much criticized by twenty-four right-wing Tory members of Parliament, so Yentob really had to bite the bullet to get this Mandela show up and running (for political reasons Rupert Murdoch's Fox Television in the United States heavily censored and de-radicalized its version of the event!).

Hollingsworth already had the productions of Glastonbury (for seven years) and Secret Policeman's Ball as feathers in his cap, among many other events, and it was he who got big names from the film, pop music, and entertainment industries to perform, present, or speak at his pop fest, including Sting, George Michael, Stevie Wonder, UB40, the Eurhythmics, Dire Straits, Eric Clapton, Sir Richard Attenborough, Harry Belafonte, Denzel Washington, Whoopi Goldberg, Richard Gere, Billy Connolly, Lenny Henry, Stephen Fry, Hugh Laurie, Harry Enfield, and Whitney Houston, to mention but a few, all of whom helped to implant a lasting image and compelling awareness of Nelson Mandela in the hearts and minds of the world with what became the biggest and most spectacular pop music protest in the world. So, too, did Jeremy Dammers of The Specials, who had already written the "Free Nelson Mandela" song in 1984.

This was a landmark pop festival that set the ball rolling for a change in the course of history and gave birth to a new kind of politics in the twentieth century. But this festival of festivals (the mother of all global pop festivals and political appeals) was a liberating turning point: a landmark political broadcast festival that no longer left the opinion forming and decision making to the politicians and political commentators, as before, but included those in the arts and entertainment world as well as the ordinary people who turned out to protest with them and made it all possible. If the British press had previously been the establishment's fourth estate—after the government, aristocracy with its royalty, and the Church of England—suddenly there was a fifth estate on the scene!

These festival people (in addition to the ANC stalwarts, anti-apartheid campaigners, and sympathetic politicians) all helped to launch Nelson Mandela on his long-distance way and powerfully so, when others were trying to keep him locked up and to diminish and discredit his political and public image. Tony Hollingsworth received bomb threats from anonymous phone callers with Afrikaner accents, but plaudits from so many widely respected others, including Archbishop Trevor Huddleston, the eminently respectable anti-apartheid campaigner, Labor leader Neil Kinnock and Liberal leader David Steel lent power to the cause, as millions of television viewers became globally aware of the great injustice done to Nelson Mandela and his ANC colleagues, becoming aware in their hearts as well as their heads—they began to feel the enormity of the bad that had been done.

And even now that Nelson Mandela is no longer with us, he remains ever-present in ghostly spirit, as two films have been released about him in London, both of which were prepared prior to his death. The London connection was always Nelson Mandela's lifeline—there is a statue of him opposite the House of Commons in Parliament Square—because it was the city that recognized him first and persistently campaigned for his release from jail more than any other, with so many expressing their outrage and lending their moral support to Mandela from a distance (my wife and I were among them in those far-distant times).

One of the two Mandela films recently released in London is based on his bestselling autobiography *Long Walk to Freedom* and called *Mandela: Long Walk to Freedom*. It is reportedly the most expensive South African movie ever made. The other film, about his second, very controversial former wife, is called *Winnie Mandela*. In the former film, Britain's up-and-coming black African actor Idris Elba—known for his roles in *The Wire* and *Luther*—has been making a big name for himself as Nelson Mandela, and obviously black South Africans have been all ears for the authenticity of the black accents of the non-African blacks acting in both these films. Idris Elba really has captured Mandela's accent and mannerisms very well indeed. Interestingly, Mandela seemed to have acquired his mock Churchillian accent—consciously or otherwise— from having had his ear constantly glued to a radio listening to Churchill's World War II speeches when, as a young man, he was a college student, as we shall see later in this book. As former British Prime Minister Tony Blair told BBC Television News at the time of Mandela's death this year, Nelson Mandela "adored" Britain and all things British, and he admired "British traditions." One can no doubt add discipline to the list of British things Mandela adored, in view of the very disciplined (and gentlemanly) way in which Mandela always conducted himself, calling for his people to be disciplined at public rallies and elsewhere.

Directed by Britain's Justin Chadwick of *The Other Boleyn Girl* fame, *Mandela: Long Walk to Freedom* is a hard film to beat, not least because it was made in consultation with the Mandela family and Foundation to ensure accuracy and with the South African film producer—Durban-based Anant Singh—planning this film for seventeen years since he first signed up Mandela for the rights to the film (Singh, a well-known South African film producer, was Mandela's preference).

There are more than one hundred black South African actors in the film and the casting of the black Londoner, Idris Elba, as Mandela, has been described as "a piece of genius," on account of Idris giving a focused, well-studied, and concentrated performance, and by all accounts mastering the unmistakable voice and self-deprecating manner and humor of Mandela very well indeed. He has said that it was an honor for him to step into Mandela's shoes.

Winnie Mandela was made in 2011 but withdrawn for a major overhaul at that time because it reportedly upset and offended too many people, including Winnie Mandela, on account of, according to its director, Darrell Roodt, its having been "emasculated in the editing process because it was trying to be honest." He told this and more to South Africa's *Mail and Guardian* newspaper, saying, "I think the producer just got nervous. There were just too many things in it that would offend too many people. It breaks your heart. You get judged even before you make the movie. I hadn't even begun shooting it and I was condemned."

Darrell Roodt is a white South African, Dutch-Afrikaner film director and writer, with a long string of South African films to his credit, including *Yesterday* in 2004, which features a black young South African mother, Yesterday, whose black miner husband gives her AIDS and then rejects her, leaving her with one ambition only, which is to live long enough to see her daughter by him, called Beauty, go to school. This film was the first to be produced in Zulu.

Perhaps Darrell Roodt should make another film called *Tomorrow* about the tomorrow that South Africa can expect now that yesterday's widely acclaimed "unifying force" of Nelson Mandela is no longer with us. Will the unifying force linger on—as Mandela has lingered on to the very last during his recent death throes prior to his demise—and will the political and racial tone that he set in South Africa remain in tomorrow's world? One is reminded by Darrell Roodt's experience that to be condemned by some people can actually be high praise indeed!

In the preface to this book I have referred to Nelson Mandela's exit from this life as a dance with death, but perhaps for a more appropriate metaphor for his demise, we should think of him having gone the distance boxing death to the final bell, rather, and never throwing the towel in prematurely, as death has had him on the ropes time and again.

This boxing metaphor comes to mind because, as anyone who has read his autobiography will tell you (*Long Walk to Freedom*, 1995, pages 225–227), he was keenly interested in boxing, in which he participated more than half a century ago, back in the 1950s, at the Donaldson Orlando Community Centre in Johannesburg where he trained "almost every evening" with professional and amateur boxers, including the black Transvaal lightweight champion, Jerry Moloi, with whom Nelson had his photograph taken when sparring with him in the ring.

Although Nelson Mandela said that he certainly "did not enjoy the violence of boxing," he was "interested in the science of it," and in particular how one used "a strategy of both attack and retreat" and "paced one's self" as a boxing contestant when a sparring partner encircled one in the ring. For sure, death has been encircling Nelson Mandela in recent months and weeks, "probing his strengths and weaknesses," leaving him and his medical team to work out their strategies of attack and defeat, pacing themselves and doing their utmost not to get knocked out of the struggle against death in the process. Before death had him on the ropes, apartheid had of course had him on the ropes a good while before that, probing his strengths and weakness, and trying to break him physically and crush him emotionally and mentally behind bars for such a painfully long time.

Always the fighter—intellectually and politically, for preference—Nelson Mandela has known when to attack, retreat, and pace himself throughout his political career, and, with his death this year, he has fought to the last without throwing the towel in prematurely. So this boxing metaphor would certainly seem to be the most appropriate for him. He has said of boxing that he liked the "egalitarian" nature of this sport, in which "rank, age, color, and wealth" are irrelevant as you are "encircling your opponent" and "probing his strengths and weaknesses."

But what can we say? What will historians ultimately say when they revisit the history of the Mandela years?

His presidency was for five years from 1994 to 1999, during which he healed the deep wounds of a racially divided nation and also charmed the outside world with a charisma all his own, widely reported to be "the Madiba magic" (Madiba is his clan name, an honorary surname taken from a Madiba clan chieftain) that consisted of a combination of self-deprecating humor, fatherly geniality, an unassuming refusal to take himself too seriously, and great compassion; but all underpinned by a shrewd and steely political acumen, not to mention an astonishing absence of bitterness or hate on account of apartheid and what it did so hatefully to him and his kind (it takes a man and a half to rise above this and in such a dignified and civilized way).

Mandela certainly knew how to woo the masses, and how to intelligently charm the leaders of other nations without brownnosing them in any way. He also knew how to forgive and forget—to forgive his former apartheid enemies without rubbing their noses in their own mire. This was his famously characteristic style that won him great respect wherever he went. So, too, was the loyalty that he had always prized: loyalty to his party, friends, and colleagues, and to those to whom he had given his word. It was often said that he would forgive most things except for disloyalty.

But had apartheid not come to an end, it is obvious that Mandela's death would have passed largely unnoticed, and the world would have been none the wiser about his many virtues or rare genius and greatness—his death would have been a very different, sad and lonely, sorry story, and a not-very-well-publicized one at that, as he died obscurely behind bars. This is all too easy to forget, as are the atrocious racial horrors of the Afrikaners' apartheid, about which most under-twenty-year-olds outside and inside South Africa will very likely know next to nothing today, and many under-thirty-, forty-, or fifty-year-olds will probably have only the vaguest recollections from their growing-up years, because they did not live those years as engaged or concerned adults.

Of course, unlike so many other leaders, Mandela had the intellect, the essential decency, the personality, and the wisdom to work all this magic and to be all things to all people—this was a virtue that came to him sincerely and naturally. He also had moral stature, so he went about his business stylishly and with genial good grace (he was a class act), cool customer and fatherly figure that he was. But, although he was in favor of collective decision making and consensual politics in theory (up to a point!), when he could not get agreement or action on urgent matters, he could and did take things swiftly into his own hands and lead from the front, making his own leadership decisions, telling others to follow and obey him, or find another leader.

Having delivered blacks from their darkest hour—and whites from an even darker hour that almost certainly would have followed—he rapidly became a friendly elder statesman and man of reason who was a symbol of hope for both sides of the black and white racial and political divide, as well as a beacon of interracial goodwill in the big wide world. But perhaps most importantly of all, he never lost his common touch with ordinary people, many of whose lives he transformed so very much for the better (but far from all lives, alas, not having a magic wand). Such was the huge humanity of the man that he also shared ordinary people's grief. It is not widely known that he jumped into his private helicopter and visited a white Afrikaner school girl dying of leukemia whose dream it had always been to meet him, or that he shook the hand of a little blind white boy who had turned out at a railway station to be one of a cheering crowd that saw Mandela off when he took South Africa's famous and luxurious Blue Train. When a white farmer shot a little black girl dead for daring to trespass on his farm in 1998, Mandela went to her home to comfort her parents and share their pain. There are many such stories about Nelson Mandela that never or hardly ever reach local or international headlines.

He didn't just reconcile blacks and whites and forgive the latter for their terrible sins of yore—he actually showed them that they could live and work respectfully together with blacks and enjoy their company if they were in a mood to do so, as he reached out and touched them all. He really made his policy of racial reconciliation work as well as could be expected in the circumstances. He did not just pay lip service to it. The fact that he achieved all this and the democratic government that came with it was miraculous to many, back in 1994 and thereafter, when he and his ANC first came to power. There is not the slightest doubt that South Africa could not have progressed so swiftly and achieved so much or gone so far in such a short space of time (Mandela's first five years) without Mandela's transforming touch.

The white man's legacy to Mandela was a country that was not just racially hateful and divided, but economically broken and administratively corrupt as well, and it needed to be mended fast, peacefully and without the civil war that was being threatened by right-wing Afrikaner white racists, not to mention the Zulu-dominated Inkatha Freedom Party and factions of the ANC that were all up for the fight. Yet he also impressed whites sufficiently well to persuade Afrikaner businessmen in their local business communities to build community centers and schools in impoverished black communities, when he was not otherwise using his celebrity status abroad to attract and keep much foreign investment to and in South Africa.

But while his legacy is brilliant, one is not so sure about his ANC party today that is not at all the party it was when he led it to become the first democratically elected president of South Africa, some twenty years ago. These days there are many criticizing the ANC and otherwise defecting from it, or no longer voting for it (including the late Nelson Mandela's good friend Archbishop Desmond Tutu); not to mention the women who are complaining that there are not enough women in the judiciary whose chief justice—a black Christian called Mogoeng Thomas Reetsang Mogoeng—is accused of not taking rape seriously (just like so many British and other Western white judges before him over the decades!).

The chief justice is described by his female critics—black and white—as an excuse-making apologist for rape, either on grounds of a woman having worn the "wrong" clothes, or of rape having been committed "accidentally." He has, reportedly, actually reduced the sentences for rape in a country that remains the rape capital of the world, even after two decades of ANC rule (one-third of African men freely and casually admit that they have raped women as a matter of course and not infrequently with a shrug of their shoulders).

South Africa is a country in which one female (chiefly a black woman or girl) is raped every four to five minutes, and the horrifying level of all-around violence against women is without doubt shameful, as is the general level of criminal and domestic violence; this, too, is alas part of the legacy of the ANC years. The chief justice is also accused of tampering behind the scenes with South Africa's widely admired constitution—there is no other like it in Africa and most other third world countries (a real feather in Nelson Mandela's hat, for preserving the legal status quo here)—and in particular it is accused of seeking to control the judiciary and make it less critical of government while also seeking to legislate in the future against freedom of the press and freedom of expression in a country in which there has always been vociferous and vibrant debate during the Mandela years. To be fair to the chief justice, he has invited his critics to show him the evidence for what he has described as their "unsubstantiated claims," so it remains to be seen how his critics will respond to this.

While the ANC is still by far the biggest South African party with the greatest number of votes, it is a party, like all others, in need of drastic reform to keep it abreast of the times, and this is a reform that it may or may not get, as we shall see before we are through with this book. But unless the party is reformed, in order to become more representative of South Africa's minorities and their parties, the country and indeed its judiciary will continue to be governed as a one-party state and one-party government on account of the single black block vote that it has in its favor, which doesn't give other parties much of a look in. But the chief concern about the ANC is that it is not the caring and fair-minded party that it was under Mandela and that it has been going downhill ever since he stepped down.

While there is no reason why the ANC should be the same party that it was in the days of Mandela—all parties change, in Britain the Labour, Liberal, and Conservative parties are not the parties they were previously or once upon a distant time— the concern in South Africa is that the party may be changing quite radically for the worse rather than the better, as is true of so many other parties worldwide.

People are asking how Mandela's legacy is affecting President Zuma's administration for the better, in view of the corruption that is by all accounts widespread among so many business and political leaders in South Africa today. The industrial unrest of miners and agricultural workers, for example, is cause for concern in events such as the injuries and deaths of workers at the hands of their own black security forces who shot and killed many of them in 2012. This unrest is likely to continue now that there has been a slump in South Africa's economic growth that is reportedly down to 2.5 percent from some 6 percent previously, as a result of the falling world demand (Chinese and European) for South African gold, platinum, and coal (mining accounts for 20 percent of the South African economy)—and, with unemployment reportedly at an alarming 25 percent, these industrial disputes are very likely to increase.

Against this less-than-cheerful background, it is no great surprise to hear that South Africa's consumer spending is down and that there is a worrying national account deficit.

For sure, there are choppy economic waters ahead for South Africa and President Zuma that are likely to be very negatively different from the "good old Mandela days." Even so, with a 2.5 percent growth rate, South Africa has a stronger economy than that of either the British or European economies, although it is falling behind the growth rates of other increasingly competitive African nations, some with more and more minerals of their own to trade with the outside world (it is a pity indeed that the South African economy is not more diversified).

The aforementioned concern that President Zuma's government is busying itself behind the scenes in an attempt to introduce unwelcome secrecy laws with which to stifle free speech and press freedom—like so many other governments before it, including the United States (let's not forget the highly publicized Wikileaks, or the Thomas Drake and Edward Snowden affairs)—aimed at curbing the public's right to know. Whether these things would have happened anyway, with or without President Zuma, is a key consideration, and we shall come to them all—and more—before we are though with this book. With the United States playing catch-up with the Chinese and others in Africa in 2013 and with President Obama having made his state visits there, it remains to be seen how much the Americans can bring freedom of speech and press freedom influence to bear (not least in view of Obama's black-African origins on his father's side), as opposed to the Chinese, who are not great fans of either of these things!

In addition to this being a book of popular history for popular interest on the occasion of Nelson Mandela's death this year, it is also a book that focuses on character studies of both the late President Mandela and the current President Jacob Zuma to see if we can get into the complicated characters and the respective natures of these two very different political leaders. When we read about them in the press or see them on our television screens, we see only a surface impression of them, but getting beneath the surface—as we shall try to do in these pages—requires some character studies of them as well.

For example, it is not widely known in North America, Britain, and Europe (and there are many things in this book that are not widely known!) that the self-taught President

Zuma—who did not have the benefit of any formal education at school or otherwise is a Shakespeare fan who is said
to love the bard's *Macbeth*, in particular, which may perhaps
give us a clue about his sensibilities and the kind of innermost
person he is; ditto the late Nelson Mandela when we look at
his favorite Shakespeare play, *Julius Caesar*, he who was "the
noblest Roman of them all."

Their preferred plays may identify them as two very
different people, but as similar characters in their passion for
Shakespeare. In his autobiography, Nelson Mandela recalls
that on one occasion in his boxing gym, Shakespeare's *Julius
Caesar* was quoted whereupon his young son (who also boxed)
asked, "Who are Caesar and Brutus?" to which somebody else
responded, "Aren't they dead?" But, in no time at all, another
person had quipped, "Yes, but the truth about the betrayal is
very much alive," and, as we know, Brutus's betrayal of Caesar
is of course an example of a truth that is very much alive today
and will very probably always be so, because that's what too
many humans do—they betray each other.

It is said that when Nelson Mandela, Jacob Zuma, and their
ANC colleagues were all locked up in the Robben Island prison
off the coast of Cape Town in Table Bay (named after Table
Mountain, flat as a tabletop—in the days of apartheid—a copy
of the complete works of Shakespeare's plays was smuggled in
to them and passed around to each in turn so that they could
read the plays at night when their prison guards were having
their meals and their evening time off to themselves. Each
prisoner was asked to underline and autograph his favorite
lines before passing the works on to the next prisoner, and
in this way Shakespeare made the rounds of the educationally conscious and diligent self-learning and self-teaching

ANC black and Indian prisoners. While it was no surprise that Nelson Mandela read the plays and marked his lines with interest, Jacob Zuma's enthusiasm and intellectual curiosity—the man being woefully far less educated than the other, if not almost uneducated—were indeed a surprise; but then, life is full of delightful surprises.

If nothing more, Jacob Zuma will in all probability go down in political history in South Africa as the one relatively uneducated, self-taught president thus far.

In addition to the profiles and biopics of Nelson Mandela and President Zuma in these pages, there are several mini-profiles and true stories of a goodly number of very minor present-day South Africans to be found here—ordinary people, not just political and ANC leaders—whose lives have been in the hands of Nelson Mandela or Jacob Zuma for better or worse and whose opinions are therefore pertinent. These are true stories from my own personal experiences and travels in South Africa for over a decade now—and from the insights and reflections that this has given me into and about its people and political leaders—so this is a freshly written book that generates its own original material and does not draw on too many academic sources or already written press reports (there are some in these pages, but not too many).

In order to write this book, I have been to the Robben Island prison (now a museum) and the Apartheid Museum in Soweto near Johannesburg in South Africa to listen carefully to what the well-informed and educated tour guides and lecturers have had to say there and to watch the very authoritative documentary films in the Apartheid Museum. I have also spoken to and interviewed black, white, and brown South Africans at all levels over a long and carefully considered period of time on different visits to their country, and I have watched with a keen eye the political and business affairs, as all South Africa watchers do.

For all these reasons, this is a very different, multifaceted, all-inclusive popular history book with a strong personal flavor, for readers who neither want (nor have the time for) a heavy academic study, nor a story that is largely written from regurgitated run-of-the-mill press and television reports with which readers are already familiar.

Whenever any author writes a book on a subject about which others are writing or have written, he or she looks to see the ground that those others have overlooked or neglected—since he or she doesn't want to merely echo what they have already said—and it seems to me from my own research and reading that the following constitutes the neglected ground, which will be covered in this book: Robben Island's effect on the character development of Nelson Mandela and President Zuma; the Shakespeare effect on these two; Nelson Mandela's amazingly magical iconic effect on his people when compared to political icons in Western and other countries, from other races; the absolutely fatal Robben Island effect on Nelson Mandela's health and life (he would doubtless have lived to be even older than his ninety-five years if it had not been for his tuberculosis that he first got in the Robben Island prison); and President Zuma's very surprising self-taught knowledge of the complete works of William Shakespeare. By considering a comparison between Nelson Mandela and well-known Western political icons, Western readers can perhaps better understand what Mandela meant to millions of black South Africans and why he had such a mighty and enduring influence upon them (given that they can understand what their icons have meant to them).

These are comparisons not usually made in other books.

While just a few quotations used in this essentially dialogic book of commentary and ideas are from the odd press report here and there—the sources and dates of which are include in the text—other occasional quotations are, as we have already seen, from the late Nelson Mandela's autobiography (also referenced in the text), while many more are from named and unnamed people in South Africa to whom I have spoken personally, or interviewed on- and off-the-record (the unnamed are unidentified in order to protect them). Other Nelson Mandela quotes included in these pages are so very well known and widely reported on many websites these days that they no longer require referencing, given that they have become part of the Nelson Mandela folklore, and I have indicated which they are.

One-third of this book is about the late Nelson Mandela and two-thirds are about South Africa under President Zuma, and this is also a book that attempts to take the temperature of South Africa and its people—while at the same time providing a guide to two black presidents with two very different histories and updated stories to be told. I have been able to write their and other related stories as a result of traveling far and wide in South Africa in and around Johannesburg, Soweto, Laudium, Pretoria, Durban, Phoenix, Stellenbosch, and Cape Town, talking to many blacks, whites, Indians, and Jews at all social levels about what they think of these very different presidents and of Nelson Mandela's nation and its prospects in his absence (and what life has been like under his and Zuma's rule).

As a former *Times* and *Financial Times* journalist in London and published author of several other books, I have been casting my pedantic but not unimaginative investigative eye on South Africa slowly but surely for a decade now, so readers will find in these pages a long and in-depth seasoned and reasoned view of South Africa, with all the detailed subtext and reading between the lines to this end. This book is not just a political text, but also a business, financial investment, and human-interest popular history text as well. Throughout this book I rely not on one point of view only—all opinions are reflected in these pages—and whatever our opinions of both Mandela and Zuma, it really is as well to remember that no other politician in the world has suffered as long and hard as Mandela (twenty-seven years behind bars and the rest) and to a lesser extent Zuma (ten years behind bars and the rest). The rest refers to suffering their years of exile and being on the run, chased from their homes, harassed, and racially segregated.

CHAPTER ONE

How Nelson Mandela Became an Icon and Got His Christian Name

NELSON MANDELA WAS educated by his black family and relatives for the purpose of—and with a view to—becoming nothing more than a minor civil servant and therefore knowing his place in the white man's wicked scheme of imperial things in the days of apartheid, leaving the grander designs of rebelling, freedom fighting, political leadership, and power politics to others.

All this is clear from reading his aforementioned autobiography, *Long Walk to Freedom*, and also from listening to others who knew him or remember him (I have done both). We know that, in his early life, he was parentally and tribally "destined" to accept an arranged marriage—from which he escaped when he rejected it and ran away to Johannesburg—and that he was also groomed to keep his nose out of racial politics. But not being one to bow to his prescribed destiny, he went his own way.

He was parentally and educationally trained to get a good Christian education and become a civil servant dealing with black people and leaving the wicked white men to do their own wicked apartheid thing—instead of which he locked horns with whites and did his own freedom fighting, presidential, and global politics thing, carving for himself and South Africa's blacks a hitherto unimagined place in history (that slowly became very imaginable indeed, painfully slowly!).

Most minor civil servants—of any race or skin color—did not do this sort of thing because they were not temperamentally or otherwise equipped for it or suited to it. They did not have the character for it, which is doubtless why Nelson Mandela did not become the minor civil servant that he was intended to become. His personal character and his nature took over from his nurture and the aims and objects of his education when he finally decided to become the first democratically elected founding-president of South Africa instead! And he became the president impressively so, which was all down to his genes and his character, and not to his family situation, in which, like many of his fellow black men and women, he could have steered clear of leadership in interracial politics and rebellion and settled for being either a cozy civil servant or lawyer. Other outstanding blacks had similarly powerful characters and personal qualities with which to become South Africa's first black president—Mandela was by no means the only one—but his was the character that eventually proved to be the most durable and capable.

Just as he rejected in his early twenties what appeared to him to be the unjust and high-handed behavior of his white Scottish college principal at South Africa's prestigious University of Fort Hare when he went there, by the same token he also rejected outright the decisions and laws of the white man's apartheid later in his life.

When Mandela and other students resigned in disgust from the students' union at the University of Fort Hare in a quarrel with the principal about their inferior food—and the college principal insisted that they could not stay in the college and complete their education unless they rejoined the students' union—Mandela walked out of the college and into the sunset, never to return!

Mandela then enrolled, later on, at Wits University in Johannesburg in order to get the longed-for university degree that he had sacrificed. But his walking away from Fort Hare turned out to be a blessing in disguise, since his law degree gave him opportunities for earning more money and advancement than the civil service diploma he would have received at Hare would have enabled him to do.

But who stands on such a small point of principle?

Well, Nelson Mandela, of course. Let's not forget that his tribal first name—Rolihlahla—meant troublemaker! Clearly, Nelson could be an impetuous and very stubborn young man of ironclad principle from the get-go!

But was he a rebel with or without a cause, or both?

It seems to me that "both" is the answer to this question, given that making such a big deal over such a small matter as college canteen food was not such a big deal and not worth sacrificing one's (educational and career) cause for such a relatively small principle.

It seems to me that Nelson Mandela was a rebel by *nature*, with or without a cause, regardless of his *nurture* (which was not to rebel at Fort Hare against his tribal family), and that it was his nature that led him to become a rebel with a very big cause in the fight against apartheid in due course. Had it not been in his nature, even before the cause came along for him personally (it was already there for the taking), the chances are that he would not have succeeded as he did.

Think of Britain's very feeble Neville Chamberlain at the outbreak of World War II—whose nature was inadequate for the task of taking on Hitler and his Nazi government and its massive army—and then think of Winston Churchill, whose nature was more than adequate, and you will get the picture. Think also of the instinctive admiration that Nelson Mandela had for Winston Churchill for standing up to Hitler, as he joined other students at Fort Hare with their ears glued to a single small radio in their dormitory as they listened to Churchill's famously stirring speeches. In my opinion, Mandela acquired his own Churchillian accent (Africa-style) subliminally in this way, and this accent lasted for the rest of his life. It is one that Archbishop Desmond Tutu imitates fondly and with glee to this day (he did so on television at the time of Mandela's death).

This is a great little true story that sheds much light on the swiftly forming character and attitudes of Nelson Mandela in his early life. In chapter two of his autobiography, Mandela tells us that he was "sabotaging" his academic career at Fort Hare "over an abstract moral principle" that he realized "mattered very little," yet he could not help himself for all that. He concedes that it was "foolhardy" for him to leave Fort Hare, but at "the moment I needed to compromise, I could not do so." And the reason he could not do so was because he "resented" his principal's "absolute power over my fate," the "injustice" of which "rankled" with him. So here we see his very stubborn and highly principled character from the beginning.

He remained obsessive about abstract moral principles, however small they may be—the mark of a truly moral and intellectual character—and he seriously resented the unjust power of others over his fate (the mark of a man whose character was without doubt his fate, determining its own fate, and would not under any circumstance suffer an unjust fate at the hands of others, however trifling or abstract the injustice and the power may be!).

For those of us who have to put up with all manner of minor or not-so-minor injustices and compromise our principles in our daily lives in order to get our jobs done or generally to survive the rough and tumble of everyday life, we detect a kind of veiled fanaticism in Mandela's character here. This is because many of us in our educational or working lives have walked away and let the college principal or our boss have his or her own way, in order not to sabotage our education, career prospects, jobs, or promotions, and to get a result, if only to repay those who have provided for us to go into higher education with our gratitude at least, or to provide for our families in life rather than to sacrifice them for our own principles (Nelson Mandela was unable to provide for his own family for twenty-seven years when he was behind bars on Robben Island).

But there was no compromising or walking away for Nelson Mandela in those days because he was made of sterner stuff. Compromise came later on, when he was in power and had more to lose, but not when he had nothing to lose. Compromise came when it made sense to do so. But he was no fanatic, for all that, and his fanatical streak, for want of a better way of putting it, had to be seriously provoked in the first place. It was more of a thinking man's intellectual streak, left to its own devices.

If we are white and not black, maybe we do not understand the depth of wounded feeling and pride that a black student feels when being overruled by a white college principal who is being unjust. Maybe we do not understand what it feels like to be humiliated. For my money, the principal was being margin-ally unjust to student Mandela (but none of us is perfect!). The principal—a graduate from Edinburgh University—did not have to make membership of the students' union a strict condition of Mandela's staying on at Fort Hare just as Mandela did not need to take the matter so personally and seriously. But then, not being black and not coming from an apartheid background, what do I know about how it was for Mandela? I just regret—as he clearly did later on—that he could not have brought himself to back down on this occasion. It is worth putting one's foot down on big points of principle, in my view, but not on little points, because there are too many of them, and life is too short.

While the young Mandela was almost certainly wrong to put his foot down as a matter of tiny principle in his dispute about the canteen food at Fort Hare, he was absolutely right, which goes without saying, to put his foot down and say enough is enough in his greater dispute with apartheid, yet he could not see the difference between the two (or, if he could, he could not help feeling as strongly about the first smaller issue as he did about the second, vastly bigger issue).

On the occasion of apartheid, when Nelson Mandela dropped out yet again—out of his job as a lawyer, out of society, and out of oppression—he did so quite rightly, because of its racially repugnant and deeply immoral treatment of its black subservient and oppressed society that was having its nose rubbed in the mire daily! In his anti-apartheid cause, it was much more to his brave and heroic credit that he dropped out in order to become an ANC political campaigner and freedom fighter instead and to show his people the way—but not without, first of all, his taking the wise precaution of completing his education and qualifying to practice law at Wits University. This time he was standing up for a massively more important and challenging principle, for which he was risking much more, including his family life with his wife and children, his freedom, and his very life that he was prepared to sacrifice for millions of people he did not know (how many of us would be prepared to do such a thing?). This was when he gave up the law to become a freedom fighter, for which he was tried and could have been convicted of treason and sentenced to death.

While Mandela's quarrel with apartheid was all too obviously monumentally bigger, more important and much more dangerous than his dispute with his Scottish college principal at Fort Hare, the point is that his character was such that he was always one to stand on his principles—large or small—and to fight for what he believed, risking all if necessary. He was never one to play safe and walk away with a shrug of his shoulders, as a great many of us do. He was no yes man. He was always concerned about the little principles as well as the large ones and, one might add, the little people as well. He went out into the streets to talk to ordinary people to find out what they were thinking and saying because, he said, he could never trust the racist South African newspapers and their publishers with their vested racist, political, and other interests to tell him the truth, the whole truth, and nothing but the truth, so he went and talked to the people directly to make up his own mind about them (he would have made a great investigative reporter), rather than believing of necessity what the papers were saying about them, especially the white man's papers.

At Fort Hare he had risked losing a good education, which he did indeed suspend and temporarily sacrifice for a tiny principle—just as in his struggle against apartheid, he risked sacrificing and losing his life when he finished up sacrificing at least twenty-seven years of his freedom instead—and in both cases this is what a great many of his fellow men would not have done, their natures and characters being very different from his (a handful would have and did so, but not many). As we have heard, in theory and on paper Nelson Mandela was supposed to have become a civil servant in a quiet backwater, dealing with his fellow blacks on behalf of his apartheid white overlords (he ticked all the right boxes for this). Not many (or perhaps any) civil servants or lawyers—black or white—would have chosen the path that Mandela chose. Had his character been different, he probably would not have done so either. So he would not have invited his personal and public fate in the way that he did, and he would not have mastered the awesome fate that his awesome character brought upon himself, while also mastering the fate of all South African blacks with it (and ironically the fate of whites, for the better, as well, not that they realized it at the time).

Without doubt one can say that *Nelson Mandela's character was his fate*—it invited his fate, brought it on, accelerated the speed of it, and finally overcame and resolved it victoriously. Fate did not have its way with him. He had his way with it.

He took his fate into his own hands and remolded it like clay to his own and his people's ends, and he did this at a time when he could just as easily have chickened out and done nothing about it, leaving it to others to see what transpired. He was fated in every conceivable way to be an oppressed victim of apartheid, like all his fellow black men and women, but with his character, he turned that fate around and remolded it big-time.

It stands to reason that those with the best character-reading skills were the ones who best read and understood the character of Nelson Mandela (and others besides, for that matter). They understood how and why his character developed over the decades, and they had the best insights into it. But one person who completely misread and misunderstood his character was Margaret Thatcher, Britain's prime minister, who wrote him off as nothing more than a terrorist who would never come to power, let alone be a president, as did many others besides in Britain, the United States, and South Africa's white community in the days of apartheid. Clearly, these guys did not have good character-reading skills. The same is true today of people who are hearing about Nelson Mandela for the first time and trying to understand his character after his recent death—they, too, need the character-reading skills and the insights.

"To be or not to be," was the question for the ever-thoughtful and ever-patient Mandela (procrastinating, like Hamlet, or otherwise being patient) when wearing his Hamlet hat, and like the intellectual Hamlet, Mandela thought very much about questions of morality, ethics, and philosophy, and he articulated them accordingly. Why not forgive South Africa's whites for their apartheid regime and reconcile the hatred between them and the blacks they oppressed? He knew, as Hamlet did, about the futility of life in general and of much misguided action in particular, and he shared Hamlet's sense of intelligent frustration on this account, but he did *not* have Hamlet's melancholy, infirmity of purpose, or feeble character that made Hamlet incapable of meeting the demands of his destiny. Mandela asked himself many times the question "to be or not to be," but not because, like Hamlet, he was incapable of being or not being, but because he was intelligent enough to consider the matter. Nor did Mandela have revenge in common with Hamlet, who revenged himself for the murder of his father; but Mandela did have Hamlet's very contemplative nature, and the "sanity and health of the whole state" was his chief preoccupation, as was Hamlet's ("something rotten in the state of Denmark" was Mandela's concern about something rotten in the state of white South Africa and, indeed, the larger world).

While Mandela did not feign madness like Hamlet, he did demonstrate, as Hamlet and Shakespeare did, that a mirror should be held up to nature, including human nature, for our careful contemplation of all its different aspects. Mandela held up his mirror—in his writings, speeches, representations as a lawyer in court, and his moral political leadership—to the need for racial reconciliation and racial equality as the only way forward. Both Mandela and Hamlet really were similar "to be or not to be" intellectuals, weighing all the pros and cons and sharing the author's art—an art invented by Shakespeare arguably more than any other English-language writer—of being mindful of every possible meaning of all the words they used, outmaneuvering and outthinking others to this end. No wonder Mandela—and his fellow prisoners on Robben Island—were, as we have seen previously in these pages, so keen to study Shakespeare when a copy of his works was smuggled into the prison. Shakespeare spoke to them in the twentieth century in the same way that he had spoken to others in the seventeenth century.

The early-seventeenth-century Hamlet was a modern thinking-man (like the twentieth- and twenty-first-century Mandela) and clearly a very philosophical, enlightened existentialist ("there is nothing either good or bad, but thinking makes it so") and also a skeptical but humane ideas-man, way ahead of his time—as, arguably, was Mandela in Africa and to a great extent globally (albeit not in the existentialist sense, given that he was a Christian Methodist). Just as *Hamlet* became the most quoted play in the Shakespeare canon, so Mandela became the most quoted political leader in Africa and also among the most quoted globally in the English language. *Hamlet* is generally regarded to be the best play in the Shakespeare canon, as is Mandela and his particular act in the African and global political affairs canon.

But when it came to the all-too-obvious infirmity of purpose of Hamlet's character, Mandela had nothing in common with Hamlet whatsoever, and he was closer to and much more like Shakespeare's Julius Caesar than Hamlet, Caesar being an all-conquering, victorious, and noble hero who was naturally born to be king, because he was naturally superior to all others—head and shoulders above the rest—not that he ever wanted or asked to be king (three times Caesar refused the crown). *Julius Caesar* was Nelson Mandela's favorite play—not *Hamlet*—and, like Caesar, Mandela refused the "crown" of presidency the first time around because he thought that he was already too old; he accepted it only under duress, and, unlike other black African leaders, he did not try to hang on to it once it was on his head. Yet Mandela, like Caesar, possessed a way of conducting himself and of carrying out his actions that suggested, consciously or unconsciously, that he ought to be a king, so others therefore treated him as such!

Being a firm believer in republican equality, Caesar resisted the temptation to be king, as of course did Mandela; but when Mandela died, his people revered him as if he were royalty, the best king they never had, as they had done prior to his death. In all these respects, we see distinct shades of Julius Caesar in the character of Nelson Mandela, and just as it wasn't events that made either man—but the destiny that each made with his own hands of the challenging events and the destiny that he had inherited—we see that both were larger-than-life characters who, for the most part, conquered and made their own fate.

So we see in Mandela, a dual Caesar-like, Hamlet-like character (two very different extremes here), with Mandela having more in common with the former than the latter, but still influenced by the Hamlet side of his character, especially where the concern over morality and revenge were concerned.

But we are also reminded by all these tried-and-true generalities of character profiling and character reading, that there are always so many more exceptions and loose ends to be tied up in individual people. We are reminded that hardly anything is ever cut–and-dried or black and white in matters of character assessment, as Nelson Mandela knew more than most. But, even so, there is much to be learned from the generality of these character studies for all that, a generality that gives us interesting pointers and valid clues to people's characters.

Mandela's character was such that, like Caesar, he heroically took on events that he could have avoided, and he eventually and stoically overcame them. And, as we have seen, he had been doing this from a young age, long before he got caught up in the struggle against apartheid—with, let us repeat, his dropping out of college, his rejecting an arranged marriage in his tribal village, his rejecting a quiet life as a civil servant or a lawyer, his narrowly avoiding the death penalty after his freedom fighting, for an alleged treason that he did not commit, his being thrown behind bars for twenty-seven years and getting tuberculosis (TB) behind bars for the first time in his life, a disease that has now finally killed him at ninety-five years of age. These were all examples of how he took these events on and invited his own fate as a direct result of the character with which he was endowed—all examples of what it was that was naturally and powerfully in Mandela's nature and character to do so, of how it was that his character was indeed his fate, not the other way around (no wonder Shakespeare took on writing about these things with his excellent character-reading schools that have so much to teach the rest of us!).

Mandela took on impossible events in a good cause that, against the odds, eventually went well for him in the end, but they could just as easily have gone badly and very nearly did so, both at his treason trial and on the remorselessly long incarceration when he spent twenty-seven years behind bars—before he became the Republic of South Africa's first founding-president, national hero, and eventual icon.

Wherever one goes in South Africa today, one hears the late and widely revered Nelson Mandela described as this republican country's closest thing to a king. One hears it said by all races (even by those whites who are or were anti-Mandela), and I have heard it several times in several different places. So the observation is in danger of becoming hackneyed. But, even so, it speaks volumes for the psychological and emotional impact that the ever-popular Mandela had on his people and the spell that he cast over them at all levels and in all racial communities, as if he were in fact a de facto king, or as if his people wished that he was their king, because they almost regarded him as such.

Not that the extraordinary spell that he cast was confined to his own country. On the contrary, it spread universally far beyond South Africa's shores. Canada made him an honorary Canadian and, as the BBC world affairs editor John Simpson has said, "Mandela was the one political leader who behaved as most of us would like all our political leaders to behave, and we find it hard to come to terms with the thought that he is leaving us" (*The Spectator*, April 6, 2013). Well, he has left us now, and it is time to come to terms with this, as we shall see in this book. We shall also see what exactly it is that South Africans and the outside world investing in, retiring to, and vacationing in South Africa have to come to terms with.

As an anti-apartheid icon—and in particular a symbol of interracial reconciliation, forgiveness, and sacrifice—Mandela will be sadly missed even though apartheid is no longer with us and is of course not sadly missed (apart from a few but highly dangerous Afrikaner cranks). It remains to be seen if the profoundly moral values and beliefs for which Mandela stood will continue to set the tone and the standard in South Africa as they always did during his reign. Some think not, and they warn of an "Arab Spring" in South Africa when all hell will be let loose, while others believe that South Africa's ANC leaders are strong, levelheaded, and mature enough to contain the situation without Mandela, as they have been doing for more than a decade already. Archbishop Tutu has rightly said that to think that black South Africa cannot govern without Mandela is to "disrespect" it.

But the situation that needs to be contained and resolved in South Africa is feared to come from the millions of South Africa's desperately poor and hungry shantytown under-class, whose patience has been wearing thin for almost two decades now in a country in which the average white family reportedly earns six or possibly seven times more than the average black family. So don't talk to South Africa's largely illiterate and predictably ignorant and potentially violent long-suffering black peasants of Nelson Mandela's ideals or of sacrifice, reconciliation, and forgiveness, argue South Africa's prophets of doom, because they are the ones who have thus far been absolutely sacrificed for the implementation of these fine ideals of Mandela's as the wealth has gone in the opposite direction, which is why they understandably crave actions and not words to relieve their desperately deprived situation from here on. Mandela's fine words have not improved their lot.

Of course it is for President Zuma to ensure that these shantytown dwellers get a new and better deal without delay now (he and his ANC colleagues, including Nelson Mandela before him, have had a couple of decades to do something about this, during which they have done nothing!), and in this sense Zuma has been handed a poisoned chalice. Although it is predicted that time is running out fast, on the other hand, this is a massive underclass that has, for the most part, not rebelled or rioted too much previously, and one with which a fair deal should not be beyond the wit of South Africa's massively better-off and filthy-rich black and white upper classes if they agree to redistribute some wealth in the direction of the poor and needy, as they urgently need to do, and as Archbishop Tutu is urging them to do. It is nothing less than amazing that South Africa's underclass has hitherto shown the enormous patience that it has, and we are reminded by this that it is not a particularly impatient or angry underclass, not that this means that it should be taken for granted any longer. We are also reminded that it is an underclass that is rapidly dying of AIDS that is keeping its numbers down, and there are those—would you believe?—who cynically hope that perhaps AIDS is the solution to the problem as it wipes out more and more people at this low level in South African society (I have heard this said with my own ears)! This is also an underclass that may settle for small rather than large mercies—as do the desperately poor underclasses in India, Pakistan, and so many other countries, for example, and as European underclasses are now being asked to do as a result of recession—but South Africa's underclass will have to be shown some mercy without delay now, because things cannot go on as they are. There will have to be affordable brick-built houses with clean water and sanitation, and better hygiene, more food, and some health services (it is of course a disgrace that this has not been on offer previously).

Because Nelson Mandela was a political leader who symbolized and actively represented all kinds of supreme, ideological, but practical ideas, in addition to and beyond the narrow politically partisan beliefs of many in his party—such ideas as forgiving our enemies but also standing up to their bullying in order to gain equality with them, such as black African self-belief and self-determination, such as the can-do ideas of never giving up and never accepting extremely adverse and unequal racial circumstances, but overcoming them rather—he inevitably became a famous icon, because of the very transforming and unifying influence that he had on his people in this way.

In these respects there are two obvious (to some but not to others) British icons to whom Mandela can be usefully compared: Margaret Thatcher and Winston Churchill.

When Margaret Thatcher died in London in 2013, she received posthumous tributes from a very gracious ANC in the best tradition of letting bygones be bygones, as Nelson Mandela preached and practiced, and some of South Africa's most notable daily newspapers paid tributes to her on their front pages, including *The Star*, which hailed her on its front page, and *The* [South Africa] *Times*, which referred to her as "an English rose." Her son, Mark, had been happy to live in luxury in South Africa in a rich suburb of Cape Town and under black South African ANC presidents that his mother, in her time, could not possibly imagine would ever come to power!

As already observed, Margaret Thatcher got Nelson Mandela and the ANC wrong in their freedom-fighting days when she described him as a terrorist and the ANC as a terrorist organization. She also said that anybody who thought that the ANC would ever come to power and govern South Africa was "living in cloud cuckoo land." Well, it was not they who were living in cloud cuckoo land! But, not being one to bear a grudge, Nelson Mandela and the ANC were quick to forgive her—along with so many others—and move on, even though she did put British investments before black people in the days of apartheid when she opposed sanctions on South Africa, while at the same time reportedly trying to talk white racist Afrikaners out of apartheid (there is not much evidence for this, but there have been some reports to this effect).

But, for all that, what Thatcher had in common with Nelson Mandela—and for which they both became icons in the eyes of their respective peoples—was that they both enjoyed land-slide victories at the polls (she three times, to become the longest-serving British prime minister), and they were both champions of freedom and democracy icons. They were also, as it happens, both God-fearing Christian Methodists. While she was not a unifying force like Mandela—on the contrary, she was very divisive—she still had plenty of other things and character traits in common with him. She was an iron lady ("you turn if you want to, the lady's not for turning"), just as Mandela was an iron man not for turning.

They also had opponents and enemies who respected them for this much, at least, if nothing else, enemies who generally conceded that they admired them even though they did not agree with them. Like Thatcher, Mandela was pragmatic in his approach to F. W. de Klerk and his apartheid enemies in order to do business with them, and later on to his white South African political opponents, just as Thatcher was pragmatic to the Soviet Union's President Gorbachev as a person that she "could do business with."

The object of making this comparison between Nelson Mandela and Margaret Thatcher—and some other great Western icons and leaders for that matter—is to give British and Western readers a much clearer idea of the kind of great political and racial icon and leader that Nelson Mandela was; to remind Western readers of what their own familiar icons are made of and how it was that the less-familiar Nelson Mandela was made of the same or very similar stuff in South Africa, and therefore meant as much to his black people as Margaret Thatcher meant to her white people and admirers in Britain and the Western world.

Not for nothing are there public squares and other places and streets named after Mandela in South Africa, with images of him on different kinds of artwork in his homeland, just as there are streets named after him in Britain and the Western world. To mention but a few, there are many Mandela street names or other place names in the UK in London, Glasgow, Harlow, Norwich, and Sheffield, as well as in France and in New York. As already mentioned, there is a prominent statue of him in London's Parliament Square outside the Houses of Parliament, just across the road from an equally prominent statue of his old enemy, once upon a time, Margaret Thatcher, inside the House. As we see, Mandela was as great an icon as any in the world at large.

Perhaps the two of them, Margaret and Nelson, will meet in heaven, since they are both Methodist Christians believing in such a place—no apartheid there, presumably!—and have some soul-searching discussions about how it was that Margaret got Nelson so wrong. Certainly, both started out as outsiders in the countries and societies in which they found themselves, she with her white face and he with his black face. And let us repeat that they were both Wesleyan Methodists—one white, one black, but supposedly equal in the eyes of their God. They were also both conviction politicians. Like Margaret Thatcher, Mandela transformed, reshaped, and redefined his nation with great courage and resolution, giving his people new hope, self-belief, and pride in being who and what they were and what they stood for (ditto Margaret Thatcher and her people in Britain), as he stood up for what he believed, as did she, and he had a lion-hearted love of his country, just as she had of hers. Both were giants—both truly extraordinary and amazing characters, like so many other icons that one can mention.

Mandela stood up against apartheid and overcame it while Margaret Thatcher stood up against Socialism, Russian Communism, the European Union, and the Argentineans in the Falklands and overcame them all! She did much to bring about the dismantling of Socialism in the United Kingdom and of Russian Communism and the Iron Curtain in Eastern Europe, just as Mandela brought about the dismantling of apartheid. She brought Communism to heel, just as Mandela brought apartheid to heel. She also brought passion into politics, as did he. In all these respects, she and he defined a new kind of leadership and purpose that saved their countries, which is why they were perceived as saviors.

Both were great and unique world leaders who won respect around the world. She was the first British and Western woman to become a prime minister in a man's world, just as Mandela was the first black male to become a prime minister in a white man's world in his country. Abroad, she was Britain, just as Nelson was South Africa abroad, both having changed the political landscapes of their countries and their times. Both were granite, extraordinary characters who burst onto the scene like events of nature! She is said to have made her people proud again—as Mandela certainly did make his people proud again—and she changed her people's thinking and the political language of their times in a dramatic new way, giving them self-belief and determination. The legacy of both to change their countries and the way in which they collectively thought powerfully drove the strong beliefs that they both possessed to a relatively successful conclusion, but were *not* able to solve the problems of their respective underclasses and their high unemployment rates for them. So they both had economic legacies that were not as powerful or successful as their ideological legacies. Here we have two national and international political icons with a great deal in common, more than we might expect. But the big thing they did not have in common was Mandela's forgiving nature and his desire to reconcile and not to divide people—Margaret Thatcher could not have been more divisive and confrontational if she had tried!—and also Mandela's lack of moral or other support for racism in this big bad world, as Thatcher had had in the days of apartheid when she was opposed to the black cause in white South Africa.

It is from iconic comparisons, and indeed character studies, such as we see in these pages (between the Mandelas, Margaret Thatchers, Jacob Zumas, and others in this world) that we all have useful things to learn, and we don't have to be political historians or students of history in order to learn them. They are things that we can usefully learn if we want to better understand those for whom we vote and how they compare and can or cannot do better on our behalf, how their characters add or do not add value to their politics, how their iconic images have the psychological and emotional effects that they do or do not have. Although there are life's usual paradoxes in such character studies and iconic comparisons—it was forever thus—there is still more to be usefully learned than that which is not very useful.

As for Britain's World War II hero and national icon, Prime Minister Winston Churchill, to whom Nelson Mandela can also be compared for meaning as much to his people as Churchill meant to his, and for similar reasons, we shall come to him in the following chapter. But, just for starters in this chapter, both Mandela and Churchill were fighters against South Africa's Dutch-Afrikaners in their time, and both were captured and imprisoned in South Africa. And both were liberation heroes—Churchill liberating his country, Western Europe, and Western civilization from Hitler and his Nazis, and Mandela liberating South Africa's blacks from the apartheid whites who were behaving like Nazis.

But apart from hearing from so many people what a massive icon Nelson Mandela was and is in South Africa, the other thing that one hears about him is the choice of his unusual Christian name, Nelson, and whether or not he was named after England's great naval officer, Lord Nelson of Battle of Trafalgar fame, with which to inspire Nelson Mandela to greatness.

For readers who have heard of Britain's Lord Nelson but never been to London, let me explain that we are talking of Britain's popular sea lord whose statue towers high over London's Trafalgar Square at the top of his lofty column in the center of the square where one will find South Africa House and England's National Gallery (for art) there, commemorating Nelson for having won the Battle of Trafalgar against the French (in 1805). The Lord Admiral Nelson was an icon like Nelson Mandela, and if Mandela is remembered and honored for as long as Lord Nelson—208 years to the present day—he will have done very well indeed! So, for that matter, will the aforesaid Margaret Thatcher and Queen Elizabeth II of England, for few in the long history of national icons can compare with the tremendously revered likes of Britain's Lord Nelson, but that's a subject beyond the scope of this book.

While Britain's World War II hero, Prime Minister Winston Churchill, can certainly be compared to Lord Nelson, few other icons can, and it is no exaggeration to say that Nelson Mandela can be compared with Winston Churchill for having stood up to and triumphed over apartheid.

As we shall see in this and other chapters, Nelson Mandela was an astonishing and very credible icon for his moral, diplomatic, patient, wise, and intellectual leadership, his resolute and never-say-die Churchillian militaristic freedom fighting, and also for his Thatcherite and gutsy strength of character as a political rather than a military leader, as well as for the charismatic spell that he cast over his people for having been their savior as he led them—like Moses leading the Jews—out of an empty and arid desert of despair.

In this way he gave his people real hope, for them to believe that they really did have and would therefore inherit a rightful place in this world to become members of mankind's global village—from which their white oppressors had cruelly excluded them and kept them in darkness—giving his people back the bright and shining light of their self-respect and self-belief that had been snatched away from them.

In all these massive respects, Nelson Mandela delivered, so there really was no credibility gap where he was concerned between perception and truth, myth and reality. He was the real deal, and the proof of this is that his solid achievements have remained solid for some two decades now; but the problem for his South African successors was and is how to take up the baton in South Africa's relay race and make those achievements last. Two decades ago, Nelson Mandela avoided a bloodbath in South Africa and achieved interracial unity; but how much longer will this last?

This brings us back to the question: Why was Mandela called Nelson, and from where did he get his first name?

His tribal first name was Rolihlahla (meaning "trouble-maker"), reminding us that sometimes there is more to a name than we realize, not that Nelson Mandela ever said in so many words that he was conscious of having to live up to his name. He apparently was not given his name for the reason of trou-blemaking. But, boy, did this troublemaker cause a great deal of trouble for the apartheid whites who caused him and his people big trouble. So, in his case, there certainly was some-thing in his name, not that we can impute anything to this because, as we know, the world is and has been full of trouble-makers who did not have a first name that meant troublemaker!

Had Nelson Mandela ever said that he had consciously lived up to his tribal name, then this choice of name would have maybe been more significant. But such a name for such a person seems to have been curiously coincidental, for all that, as does his victorious Nelson Christian name. The precise meaning of his new name, Nelson, that was given to him in place of his tribal name is generally agreed to be "son of Neil—whosoever Neil may have been once upon a distant time—but Britain's Admiral Lord Nelson was the son of an Edmund (not a Neil), an English vicar born in Cambridge who died in Bath in Somerset, and Mandela's father was certainly not called Neil either! Interestingly, the O'Neills are chiefly from

Scottish and Ulster (Northern Irish Protestant) stock, so there are plenty of sons of Neill in those countries, not that Admiral Nelson or Nelson Mandela were from such stock.

While there are dozens of other less-famous people called Nelson in different parts of the world, the name remains unusual, and now there are fans of Nelson Mandela naming their children after him.

But why should anybody care whether Nelson Mandela was named after Britain's great and victorious sea lord or not?

Well, most people don't care, but they are nevertheless intrigued by this unusual choice of name for him, as was Nelson Mandela himself, because he would not have mentioned it in his autobiography otherwise.

Of course, he would have been inspired to greatness regardless of his name—with or without an intended reference to the famous Lord Nelson of the aforesaid Battle of Trafalgar—but to get the gossipy significance of his Christian name out of the way in this, the first chapter of this book, we look at how he came by it.

We also blow kisses to the late Nelson Mandela in this chapter, if we are of a mind to do so on the occasion of his death—as of course do millions in South Africa and the world at large—which is exactly what Lord Nelson's sea captain did to Lord Nelson at the point of death, as did the rest of England thereafter.

Blowing kisses to Nelson Mandela seems a nice way to start a book about him and his current successor President Zuma, and England's Admiral Nelson is supposed to have said on the warship on which he was dying in the English Channel, "Kiss me, Hardy, kiss me." One likes to think of Nelson Mandela being kissed by his nearest and dearest at his demise this year.

Had the English lost their crucial Battle of Trafalgar, it is not impossible that they would be speaking French to this day, as would perhaps the United States of America and the rest of the English-speaking world, as would Nelson Mandela and his people before he died (they might otherwise have all been speaking Spanish had the English and Sir Francis Drake not defeated the sixteenth-century invasion fleet of the invincible Spanish Armada sent by King Philip of Spain in 1588).

Had the imperialist French (or Spanish) conquered England and the rest of Britain, the world and South Africa probably would be a very different Spanish-speaking place today, but as things turned out, the English won their wars against both these nations (ditto their Battle of Britain against Hitler's Germany during World War II).

By the same token, had Nelson Mandela lost his struggle against apartheid, all South African blacks would very likely be speaking Dutch these days, or the Afrikaners' version of the native tongue of their ancestors.

While England's Lord Nelson had only one arm—which was amputated on board a warship after a skirmish on the Spanish island of Tenerife when, only half an hour after having his arm removed by his surgeons, the Admiral returned to the gunfight that had caused the loss of his arm!—by comparison, Nelson Mandela had both his arms. But it is true to say that he had one arm tied behind his back in the odds that he fought against apartheid, which was not a fair fight for him or for his people.

Later on in his career, when Lord Nelson died of gunshot wounds on his HMS *Victory* warship before the Battle of Trafalgar was won, as we have heard, he was famously supposed to have whispered to Thomas Hardy, his friend and captain of the ship, "Kiss me, Hardy, kiss me," because he knew that he was on his way to the next world, just as Nelson Mandela is on his way now.

Hardy knelt down and kissed Lord Nelson gently as a child, once on his cheek and once on his forehead, in the spirit of the age, and, for all anybody knows, Lord Nelson, whose faint voice was rapidly shrinking and disappearing with his last breath in his mouth (as was Nelson Mandela's at the end of his life), might perhaps have whispered at low-volume "kismet, Hardy, kismet,"—meaning "fate, Hardy, fate" (kismet is the Turkish word for fate). But whichever of these whispering utterances that he made, Lord Nelson got his kisses and went on his way to his hereafter, whereupon his body was put into a cask of brandy mixed with camphor and myrrh in order to preserve it on the return sea journey to England. To this day, some British naval officers and sailors refer to "toasting the Nelson" when downing a glass of brandy (no doubt there will be all sorts of toasts to and anecdotes about Nelson Mandela in the fullness of time, since this seems to be the fate of most icons).

There are even suggestions of British naval officers and ordinary sailors making another toast that is referred to as "tapping the Nelson" when downing a glass of brandy because the barrel of brandy in which Lord Nelson's body was put to preserve it at sea was said to have been regularly tapped by ordinary seamen who needed a drink after such a nerve-racking, massively exhausting and bloody battle, even though the sea lord's dead body was still marinating!

As we see, Lord Nelson's final kismet—his ultimate fate—was well and truly sealed by a French bullet and a cask of brandy, and this is the seafaring man that was a monumental icon of British history after whom Nelson Mandela may or may not have been named.

These intriguing anecdotes about the great men of history—great icons, no less—are well worth contemplating if we are to understand how our history was made and by whom and in what way, what the outcomes and results were, and the directions in which we are therefore pointed today. This is as true of South Africa and its black and white leaders in the twentieth and twenty-first centuries as it was of the West and its white leaders previously. These are all anecdotes that bring with them much seminal thinking, intellectual curiosity, and food for thought, and in the long reach of time, there are important things to be learned from the history-makers whom different races have followed, which is why, for example, there are important things to be learned from the differences in character between the Churchills, Stalins, and Hitlers of this world, as well as between Nelson Mandela, President Zuma, and their white apartheid predecessors. They are all part of history's rich tapestry and pattern, in which there are parallels between different leaders that are worthy of consideration, with some parallels more relevant than others. Anyone who writes about these matters and does not cause his or her readers to think about these matters is not a thinking writer, and who wants to read writers who do not provoke thought?

As we have heard, left to his own devices, Nelson Mandela may have settled for being a minor civil servant; his first and only ambition once upon a time was to be a civil servant or a lawyer. But apartheid did not leave him to his own devices. So, cometh the man, cometh the hour, and not least because he had the character for it, if not the ambition. In contrast to Lord Nelson's fate, Nelson Mandela's ultimate fate may very well have been sealed in advance, without his earlier knowledge. It was probably sealed by his imprisonment on Robben Island (meaning "Seal Island") at the hands of his white racist oppressors during the apartheid era, which resulted in tuberculosis for him, as a result of his cold and damp prison cell (or other prisoners, or from his hard labor in a limestone quarry where he was forced daily to relentlessly sledgehammer away at a mountain of hard stone). This was a disease from which he then proceeded to suffer in later years, with its lingering lung infections that recurred until the day he died, reportedly of an interrelated lung infection, pneumonia, and heart failure.

It was also during his time on Robben Island that Mandela's aging mother and his eldest son died—both in 1968, his son in a car crash—but he was not allowed by the harsh, mean-spirited, and very spiteful apartheid government to go to either of their funerals. This must have hurt him deeply and saddened him terribly (he had another son who died of AIDS after Nelson's release from jail later on). Can you imagine being behind bars when your mother and son die and not being allowed to go to their funerals?

This was all part of the price that Nelson Mandela paid for standing up to apartheid, but stand up to it he did, triumphing over it after twenty-seven long years behind bars.

The other part of the price he paid was his tuberculosis, which contributed to or caused his death at ninety-five years of age.

But to come back to the original question: What to make of the choice of Nelson Mandela's English first name?

How did he come by it, and why was he given it?

Nelson Mandela was given his first name by a black female school teacher at the first missionary primary school that he attended in South Africa when he was a young child.

The school that gave the young Mandela his Christian name was a British Christian missionary village school in the Eastern Cape province where all black pupils were given the Christian names of white men and women. Only the brightest and best black children became pupils in these schools.

When Mandela referred to the choice of his name in his autobiography, he made it clear that he had no idea why the name Nelson was chosen for him, but he also said that he did wonder if he had been called after Britain's Lord Nelson.

So the fact that he wondered about it in passing and put it into his autobiography is not insignificant, even though to wonder about it is certainly no big deal.

Because his black mother, Fanny—the only one of his father's several black wives who was a Christian—had become a Christian convert and had been given her Christian name by her local church, her son Nelson was baptized in a local Wesleyan Methodist Church with its own schoolhouse on the other side of the hill from Qunu, the village in which he lived. This is a village to which, before he died, Nelson Mandela made return visits back to his original roots, and where he has now been laid to rest. His grandson Mandia is the tribal chief of that village today where, once upon a distant time, the five-year-old Nelson Mandela herded cattle and had the lowly ambition only to be a stick-fighting champion!

The local schoolhouse in Mandela's day was a single room to which he began to go daily at seven years of age in 1925. It was on his very first school day that his teacher—Miss Mdingane (perhaps the Mdingane family knows why he was called Nelson?)—gave him and the other black children their Christian names. Having been born in 1918 at the end of World War I in Europe, the young Nelson Mandela was all set to become an educated, English-speaking Christian gentleman, and he found that this suited him well.

As he said, long before he died, education—as the great engine of personal development and growth—is what determines whether, for example, the son or daughter of a peasant or a farmer can become a medical doctor or the president of a nation, or whether the son of a mineworker can become the chief executive of a mine. It was in this belief that Nelson Mandela happily and hopefully embraced his Christian education and the Christian name that came with it. Without education, most of the uneducated or informally educated are lost forever (there are obvious exceptions, such as President Zuma, but for most people, this is true). So Nelson Mandela was very pleased to receive his education in his Christian missionary day school, from which he went to a boarding school afterwards and then to university. As soon as he got his Christian name, he and all the other children were immersed in a British education with all the British culture and ideas that went with it—it was their magic moment, receiving their names that were handed out to them like sweets—and it was this old colonial culture and its ideas that also got them started in their eventual mastery of and fluency in the English language, as a result of which Nelson Mandela remained a great fan of Britain and the British for the rest of his life.

But this did not prevent him from observing that British and other whites when he was in his first school—in the early twentieth century—were either unable or unwilling to pronounce the black African names or "considered it uncivilized to have one." But, for all that, he remained forever pleased that he received an English-language education, not least because of the advantages that it brought him, enabling him ultimately to become a lawyer and a world-renowned statesman, in addition to becoming the first democratically elected founder-president of today's Republic of South Africa.

It was his English first name and the education and culture that came with it that determined his fate and influenced his character development to a large extent, as indeed did his mother Fanny's conversion to Christianity. He could not have become a lawyer or the global spokesman for his people without it. Nor would he have got Britain's culture of post-1960s liberal-minded, democratic, and politically and socially reforming ideas without it, including its culture of free speech and human rights. Perhaps he would not have gotten his patient store of toleration without it. He could not have advanced himself or expressed himself so well in the world at large without any of this. So we see that his fate was suddenly set in cultural stone for the better by his English education, but that later on his fate was changed for the worse by the racist miseries of Dutch-Afrikaner apartheid.

For Nelson Mandela to have been coincidentally given the first name of such a great Englishman as Admiral Lord Nelson before he actually became a great man himself was indeed a nice and very curious touch. But the extent to which his inspirational name had a subliminal effect on his mind and his strength of purpose and character thereafter is impossible to say (in my opinion very little) and not least because he himself suggested no such thing in his autobiography. Probably his name was the luck of the draw, or his school teacher's favorite name that she reserved for him for some reason, not that at seven years of age it occurred to him to ask. He was too busy thinking about getting himself educated. Probably almost any name would have suited him fine.

Obviously whatever his name had been, here was a young man who was capable of extraordinary and great things, with or without an extraordinary or inspirational name. His name was given to him apparently randomly, as were all the other black kids' names. If his teacher had reserved the Nelson name especially for Rolihlahla, because she thought it suited him better, or because she liked the idea of naming him after the great and victorious British naval officer, we have no idea. What we do know is that his parents had deliberately called him Troublemaker (and given that this was before they had any idea whether this was an apt name for him or not, presumably they hoped that he would live up to such a name and cause trouble, as he certainly did!). We also know that Lord Nelson and Nelson Mandela were, as things turned out, both troublemakers, the former for the French and the latter for the Dutch-Afrikaner apartheid regime.

What we have here are two extraordinary coincidences. Here was a boy called Troublemaker who turned out to be a troublemaker and here was a boy named after such a great and inspirational man as Lord Nelson who turned out to be a great and inspirational man.

Explain that if you can! However, before we finish with Mandela's identity and his image in this chapter, there is just one more thing to be looked at regarding his being an icon— in this case a sex icon!

Certainly he knew how to charm the ladies, and there was never any doubt that the ladies wanted to be charmed by him.

He has admitted that he sowed plenty of wild oats before marriage.

But he was not such a very great sex icon thereafter, having been preoccupied with so many other deadly serious and distracting matters. However, he had three wives in addition to at least one heartthrob who turned down his offer of marriage in 2013, according to her son. But having been forcibly separated from his second wife, Winnie, (and all other women besides) by so many years behind bars, for most of his adult life (perhaps the best years of his life), he was obliged to live like a monk, which is why he did not marry his third wife until much later on, when he was an old man.

After his release from jail in 1990, one can say of Nelson Mandela's sexual conduct that it has been, as in all things, modest and quietly unassuming in his romantic conquests, and this, of course, has been part of his attraction to a certain kind of woman.

Unlike President Zuma—or Italy's Berlusconi for that matter—Nelson Mandela always showed moderation. He was not a gleeful or boastful womanizer and philanderer—definitely not his style—but he is reported as saying that he "can't help it if the ladies take note of me. I am not going to protest" (*The Guardian*, April 1, 2013).

But compared to many political and other leaders, he did not have a great many different female friends or mistresses, and he was not a polygamist (as was his father) with several wives and girlfriends at once. Nor did he have girlfriends half his age (in contrast to Italy's President Berlusconi), or a widely publicized premarital or extramarital sex life (as in the case of Britain's Prince Charles and so many others besides), and he has not let sex interfere with his presidential duties (as did America's President Clinton with Monica Lewinski!). So, as sex icons go, it seems reasonable to conclude that the late Nelson Mandela had been a bit of a tempest in a tea pot!

Yet he was a celebrated charmer who did not lose the habit of attracting women in his old age, and the woman who is supposed to have turned down his offer of marriage before he married his third wife (Graça Machel, the former wife of President Samora in Mozambique, whom Mandela married on his eightieth birthday in 1998), is said to be the late Amina Cachalia who died in 2013 at eighty-two years of age. Her son Ghaleb tells us that his mother politely turned Mandela down when he asked for her hand in marriage in the 1990s.

Ghaleb's mother was a prominent anti-apartheid activist who had visited Nelson Mandela in Pollsmoor Prison, as a result of which he became her friend and a friend of her family, including her husband Yusef. But when Yusef died in 1995, it is claimed that Mandela, who was divorcing his second wife, Winnie, at the time, asked for Amina's hand in marriage, but that she turned him down because "she wanted to honor the legacy" of her marriage to Yusef, who had been fifteen years her senior and "the love of her life."

Her witty son tells us "perhaps after getting rid of one old man, she didn't want to take another on!" But he also reckons— in his book *When Hope and History Rhyme*—that there were "romantic interludes" between Mandela and his mother in the 1990s.

However, looking at Mandela's love life throughout his long career that was so rudely interrupted by apartheid, it seems obvious that "romantic interludes" were the best that the great man could hope for, especially during the most sexually active period of his life, and even as an older man as well, given that he did not blaze a sexual trail like some we could mention (and have mentioned!). He was always the great moral leader above all things, a moral giant no less. And in this respect he was not at all like his namesake Lord Nelson who had his mistresses, in addition to his wife, but who did not have as many wives as Mandela.

It was hardly surprising that Nelson Mandela and other educated South African blacks wanted fluency in the English language, not the despised Afrikaner-Dutch language. As we have seen in this chapter, there are plenty of very good reasons why Nelson Mandela became a national icon, leading his people out of the tyranny and oppression of apartheid, not unlike Moses leading the ancient Israelites out of the desert in the years before Christ, away from the tyranny and oppression of ancient Egypt to give the Jewish people a spiritual and eventually an actual homeland in Israel. So here again is another icon with whom Nelson Mandela can be compared!

To compare Mandela with Moses is by no means exaggerated and not at all difficult to understand if we know about the interracial history of icons and how they are made (if we do not know, then it's well worth finding out); and unlike Moses—the veracity of whose life and achievements have been disputed by archaeologists and others—the veracity of Nelson Mandela's life and achievements are beyond dispute and far better recorded in the twentieth and twenty-first centuries than was Moses's life in those distant times before Christ.

As the savior of his people, Nelson Mandela is every bit as credible and verifiable as both Moses and Lord Nelson as national icons, and we do him an injustice if we do not record this for history.

What sped him on his way more than anything else was, without doubt, his English education and the freedom-loving democratic culture that came with it. What would have held him back and quite possibly silenced him in the outside world was a Dutch-Afrikaner culture and language. A Dutch-speaking and narrow-minded Dutch-Afrikaner education and culture is what he and most other educated and ambitious South African blacks did not want, for obvious reasons entirely to do with the detested apartheid, not to mention the Dutch language and culture not being a global language or culture like the English language—the twentieth century's voice of freedom, democracy, and reason in this big wide world, in which Nelson Mandela and his ANC colleagues were determined to make themselves heard.

Nelson Mandela and his black brethren did not want the rigidly and tyrannically imposed "separateness" (*apartheid* in Dutch) of the Dutch-Afrikaners. Mandela and his brethren wanted the liberalized multiculturalism of the British and their Christianity that was so very different, much more liberal-minded and conscience-stricken, less racist and much more consistently reforming (see the following chapter) than the Christianity of the Dutch Reform Church out of Holland and in South Africa that blessed the evils of apartheid in the name of its God!

Having got himself unusually named by chance, quite possibly but not definitely after the great British sea lord Admiral Nelson—and almost certainly not knowing, as a child back then, the "kiss me, Hardy" legend from the Battle of Trafalgar—Nelson Mandela will have been kissed goodbye this year, not only by his nearest and dearest who attended him at his bedside when he died, but metaphorically by millions of his fans throughout the world and also Africa, blowing their kisses to him from afar.

It would be nice to think of so many people kissing him goodbye. Hence this chapter at the outset of this book that blows kisses to him and his memory in the immediate aftermath of his death, as another nice touch with which to start this story about him and the South Africa that he created and has now left behind, having founded it almost two decades ago in 1994.

CHAPTER TWO

An Agonizing Political History

WHILE THE LATE Nelson Mandela's global image was such that he almost certainly needed no introduction to most people, the agonizing detail and suffering of his political life and history is not so well known, unless one has been to South Africa to visit the museums and places of learning there where one can indeed learn these shocking details (if one speaks up and asks enough questions); or unless one has read his autobiography and the recent histories and documents on the subject of apartheid, which readers are well advised to do if they have not done so already, should their appetites be whetted by this book, as hopefully they are.

There are even white South Africans today who are not familiar with too many of the details, either because they don't want to know, their parents or grandparents have been too ashamed to tell them, or their schools have not taught them. So they see no evil, hear no evil, speak no evil! Generally speaking, and with few exceptions, the older Afrikaner generation does not want to be reminded of or to admit to its past sins, and it does not tell its children and its children's children about any of this. On the contrary, the older Afrikaner generation hushes it up, and does not take its children or its children's children to visit the places where they can learn the history for themselves.

Certainly, to understand the agonizing political history, one needs to read the books or to visit such places as the Apartheid Museum and the former Robben Island prison (now a museum) in South Africa, and talk to the guides and the staff there about the ghastly things that happened under apartheid and what happened to Mandela and Zuma when they were behind bars. When one does so, one notices that there are not infrequently American and Continental European tourists flooding into these places, including plenty of African and Caribbean/West Indian Americans.

One can otherwise refer to South Africa's Truth and Reconciliation Commission for the "profound apology" that the white Afrikaner former exponent of apartheid, F. W. de Klerk (meaning "the clerk"), has made for his government's disgusting system of apartheid when he was the last president of his white man's South Africa, before Nelson Mandela and his ANC came to power in 1994, for which both men were awarded Nobel Peace Prizes in 1993.

De Klerk, of French Huguenot origin, has made it clear—not only to the Truth and Reconciliation Commission but in the media also—that apartheid was "morally reprehensible" and "indefensible" for "trampling on the human rights of people" (in other words, apartheid was morally repugnant!). Reportedly, he claims to have some colored (not black) mixed-race blood in his family's veins many distant moons ago, not that one would think so looking at him today, for he is whiter than white!

He reckons there was "no animosity" between him and the late Nelson Mandela when the latter took over as president from the former, and that they remained "close friends" who phoned each other on their respective birthdays (thanks, of course, to the superior morality and astonishingly forgiving and unbitter nature of Nelson Mandela).

Even compared to India's Mahatma Gandhi—who preached nonviolence but not the racial forgiveness of the oppressors by their victims—Mandela arguably comes out as the greatest moral influence in world politics of all time, given that what he preached averted an expected racial bloodbath when he and his fellow blacks found themselves in the driving seat after they had gotten rid of their apartheid oppressors. It is also the case that Gandhi was himself among those who felt racially superior to South Africa's blacks, whom he described as inferior in his writing, and there are plenty of blacks in South Africa today who have not forgotten this.

Unlike Gandhi, Mandela had many better political skills and leadership qualities in addition to his moral qualities, and Gandhi, as we know, did not manage to avert a bloodbath after partition in India in 1947 when there was a ghastly bloodbath between Hindus and Muslims after the British left, the racial and religious prejudices, hatred, and politics of which have continued to this day, without any divide and rule help from the British, who can no longer be falsely blamed for racist and separatist attitudes and hostilities between both Muslims and Hindus in India. With the history, traditions, and mindsets of the latter deeply immersed in a morally reprehensible caste system (with its "untouchables" still very much untouchable)—for which Nelson Mandela never did and never would have had any time with his superior morality—India, Pakistan, and Bangladesh have not, alas, moved forward racially or morally, as has South Africa under Mandela. One doesn't have to have read Rudyard Kipling to know about these things. All one needs to do is to travel far and wide in India and keep one's eyes wide open, as I have done, and to have plenty of Indian and Pakistani friends in London, as I have, to know perfectly well that Hindus and Muslims are racially prejudiced toward each other and that most of them were not influenced for the better by Gandhi, as most South Africans and so many others in the world at large were influenced for the better by Mandela. It seems unlikely that Mandela could have achieved the racial harmony that Gandhi failed to achieve in India, had the former been confronted by fanatical Muslims (and also Hindus) rather than fellow Christians in South Africa. But Mandela was a much more practical and less mystical leader than Gandhi, and Mandela arguably made more political sense to his racial opposites and others than Gandhi ever did to his. Gandhi also wrote that South Africa's blacks were racially inferior to Indians and Brits (for which many black South Africans are not great fans of Gandhi to this day). In my opinion, Mandela had many more political and leadership qualities than Gandhi, who was more of a preacher than an active leader, whereas Mandela was both a preacher/rainmaker as well as an active and politically more astute and worldly leader than Gandhi was. Of course, Gandhi is still an icon to many (but not too many) in India, but he is nowhere near as much of an icon as is Mandela, and he did not achieve as much for his people as did Mandela.

But where did Nelson Mandela's leadership qualities come from?

At the beginning of his adult and political life, these qualities most probably came from Mandela's formative years of childhood, as usual, but he also had many epic and dramatic rebirths later on in his life that were so contrasting and character developing and character renewing in the passage of time.

These rebirths ranged from university graduate and lawyer to husband, father, anti-apartheid campaigner and activist, freedom fighter and then a prisoner behind bars for a staggering twenty-seven years before finally rebirthing as a Nobel Peace Prize winner, founding-president of South Africa, and a world statesman. Gandhi—also a lawyer like Mandela, both of whom practiced in South Africa—never had so many transforming and character-developing or renewing experiences and rebirths with so many lessons to learn for the better (lessons that Mandela learned well).

Nelson Mandela said of his time behind bars that, in prison, one comes face-to-face with time, which is terrifying, but in his case one suspects that he also faced his true monumental self and all his inner strengths and weaknesses and learned them well—face-to-face with the inner man, the contemplation of which he was so eminently capable.

Obviously twenty-seven years behind bars is a monumentally formative and born-again experience, and it doesn't take much imagination to understand the agony that had to be endured during this time.

Notwithstanding the agony, one learns a great deal of patience and worldly wise cunning, scheming, and tactical thinking in order to survive a prison life at the hands of one's brutal prison guards. So it is not hard to imagine how Mandela's character had doubtless been shaped by his painfully long prison sentence, in such a way that enabled him to perform better as the president of South Africa when the time finally came after such a long time behind bars. A significant amount of psychological, emotional, inner-resource, and intellectual flesh has been put on Mandela's bones by his prison experiences—much more than on Gandhi's bones and also much more than on Jacob Zuma's bones, because the latter arrived on Robben Island with learning difficulties and deficiencies that Mandela did not have and also spent seventeen fewer years in prison than Mandela.

While, as we shall see in this chapter, Jacob Zuma was certainly strengthened by his prison experiences, it was in a very different way from the deep-thinking manner in which Mandela was strengthened. While Jacob Zuma learned how to think and to improve his reading and writing in prison, Nelson Mandela had no need of such learning because he was already a thinker, reader, and writer, but he did contemplate and "think" much more than he might have done otherwise, and his character and intellect developed much more in consequence. He also read a great deal of Shakespeare. The educational head start that Mandela had earlier in life put him streets ahead, as he went up through the gears, while Zuma, by all accounts, was still finding his educational way in first gear (which was all to the good because he had not had the benefit of any gears previously, not having been formally educated).

The psychological and emotional consequences of these two character-changing and character-forming personal development experiences of both these leaders were not to be underestimated for either man; with all the extra time that they had on their hands, they could think and learn about their political beliefs and philosophies and get their thoughts together about how best to articulate their beliefs and the values for which they stood.

Twenty-seven years behind bars for a sophisticated thinker like Mandela, as for anyone, certainly must have been agony, yet he bore no visible scars that anyone could see. There was, amazingly, no bitterness in his golden heart. On the contrary, he somehow managed to rise above his agony and pain and emerge immune.

He would have used all the psychological insights, charm, and charisma that he could muster to get the best out of his coldhearted guards, being careful not to give them the slightest excuse for treating him even more badly than he was being treated already. These were all skills that made him a better president when the time came to negotiate with statesmen all over the world, as well as with his own ANC leaders and members, as well as with black African neighboring countries and with his former apartheid enemies in the white community. His character would have been changed for the better and strengthened in all these respects in a very considerable way. When Nelson Mandela first arrived on Robben Island and a prison warden threatened him with physical abuse, saying that he was going to crush him physically and mentally, Nelson soon told him that in the event of physical abuse, he would have the despicable man in court, beyond the prison walls. On the other hand, Mandela behaved well to the guards who behaved well to him, so he was learning how to box clever, and this was a learning curve that served him well in later life when he entered politics again, after his release from jail, with twenty-seven years of boxing clever behind him.

Both Mandela and Zuma were known for their charisma and charm, the easy habit of which they will also have learned how best to put to good effect in prison.

Both Mandela and Zuma were thrown behind bars on Robben Island in the 1960s, when British and Western European jails were getting softer, easier, and more civilized for criminal prisoners in the United Kingdom and Europe. But not so in the Robben Island jail off the coast of Cape Town.

Because this former prison is a museum today, visitors can spend time viewing the corridors, cells, and grounds—it is a vital visit for anyone seriously interested in knowing what happened in the days of apartheid and how harsh and cruel the conditions were in this notorious jailhouse—including a visit to the most famous cell of all, Nelson Mandela's.

His was a damp, cold, soul-destroying, and dehumanizing cell in a harsh and severe prison in which there was seriously insufficient food and woefully inadequate medical care, where prisoners were subjected to backbreaking and grueling labor daily and not infrequently verbally and physically bullied and brutalized by their racially arrogant and seriously callous and racist white prison guards.

One cannot visit this sad, sorry, and grimmer-than-grim place without reflecting on how it must have shaped the characters of so many of South Africa's ANC leaders, not just Nelson Mandela, but three out of four South African presidents who were incarcerated there.

There was yesterday's Nelson Mandela and Kgalema Motlanthe (the relatively unheard-of caretaker president who stepped in to hold the fort before Mbeki took over as president after Mandela departed) and also today's President Zuma.

One can well imagine the deep sense of dislocation and mighty loss of freedom that came like an equally mighty sledgehammer shock to the system to them all, after being shoved behind the Robben Island bars like this.

The influence of Robben Island in shaping the future leaders and leadership of both South Africa and the ANC with which we are familiar today is all too clear. It was a place from which one would emerge for better or worse, and, in most cases, these ANC leaders emerged, astonishingly, for the better, to judge from their postprison political and personal conduct.

But what of the precise details of the agony that they learned to endure and survive there? How agonizing was it?

What we can say of the absolute horror that they all shared was that they endured extremely harsh conditions to which they had to accustom themselves without letting those conditions break their spirits or their hearts and without losing their dignity (as their surroundings were clearly designed to do).

These conditions reportedly included: not infrequently sleeping on cold and damp stone floors in the single cells without beds or warm blankets, as and when the guards saw fit; enduring hard labor in a quarry pit; being ravenously hungry but given only just enough food and water for survival; being intimidated, bullied, and mistreated by prison guards both physically and psychologically; being monitored round the clock and kept in isolation for any misdemeanor dreamed up on a pretext by white racist guards; being at a loss to know what one had done wrong, other than standing up for one's human and civil rights and racial equality in the struggle against racist apartheid; being sick of heart and low of spirit and soul but having to grit one's teeth to rise above all this; being lonely, depressed, or in despair; and having virtually no mercy or kindness shown toward one.

How much more agony does one need or can one take?

How does one not become bitter on account of all this?

All of the above varied depending on whether prisoners were in the single cell area (as Mandela was) or in dormitories in the general section of the prison, but in whichever part they were, when you consider the collective impact of all this on prisoners and how it affected them all very differently—breaking some prisoners but not others, poisoning the hearts, souls, and minds of some but not others, strengthening or weakening some—you can see that this was an agony that would make or break them.

Clearly and astonishingly it did not break Nelson Mandela or President Zuma. But if it actually made them by hammering them into an even sturdier shape than previously, it was a hammering that they could have done without, spiritually, mentally, emotionally, physically, and psychologically.

Obviously both these men must have had some pretty amazing inner resources to endure all this—Nelson Mandela for some twenty-seven years and Jacob Zuma for ten years.

But there was—ironically—an unintended and very positive intellectual, educational, and political gain to being in Robben Island for ANC and other anti-apartheid freedom fighters, for whom Robben Island was the making of many, especially those like President Zuma, having had no formal education when he arrived. But this was a gain that was only possible if one could endure all the agony without being beaten by it, if one could learn to live with the agony as ANC leaders generally managed to do, without letting it scar or embitter them, as with common consent, they did not let it do.

If one was in the general section of the prison rather than the single cells, it really did become a kind of regular college of adult education, for political prisoners who had a lot of time in the evenings for much more thinking, discussing, and debating among each other than would have been the case otherwise, which was the upside of prison life for them. Prisoners in the general section had time for deeper thinking, speculation, and discussion at unofficial secret seminars about the pros and cons of their cause, how best to reinforce it, and so on. In this way they thought things through with increasing clarity of mind and purpose, with the lesser educated learning from the better educated, the inexperienced and less able learning from the experienced and the more able, the more articulate and the more professional teaching and influencing the others a great deal; all of which meant that, when the time came for their release, they were far better educated, intellectually prepared, and informed than they were when they first went into jail! Many if not most came out more thoughtful, intellectually confident, and better politically educated than before, especially Jacob Zuma, who learned a great deal from his better-educated and more articulate peers, whose company he would not have kept otherwise, and without whom he would not have had this golden opportunity to learn in the educational hothouse of Robben Island!

In this way, with all these political thinkers and learners under one roof, Robben Island could not fail to become an unofficial college of higher education for adults who were no longer students or had never been students in the first place. In all consideration, it seems that far from being weakened by their soul-destroying incarceration, the prisoners became more resolved, strengthening themselves physically and intellectually, as well as strengthening their political networks and organizations beyond the prison gates (through visitors if they were in the general section of the jail that was less scrutinized by the guards).

The learning that these prisoners did in secret was at unofficial night schools when their guards were looking the other way or enjoying their own leisure time—prisoners were constantly monitored otherwise—and in this way these prisoners managed to further their people, management, and communication skills, as well as their underground networks of information for the organization of their political campaigns, political parties, and factions beyond the prison gates.

By all accounts, the prison authorities in Robben Island blew hot and cold on the subject of this kind of learning, sometimes allowing the prisoners to educate themselves freely, other times not, depending on the alternating degrees of racism and vacillating moods of the different guards in question at any given time, and also depending on whether prisoners were in isolated single cells. So the goalposts were always moving, with prisoners being arbitrarily denied their opportunities to study and lecture each other one moment, but allowed to do so the next!

It is said that while Jacob Zuma had left school without educational qualifications, it wasn't because he couldn't read or write, but because he went to a rough-and-ready school that did not prepare black children for exams, which is why he did not formally finish. The same was true in postwar Britain in the secondary old schools where children were not prepared for Senior Cambridge or O-level examinations that they did not need to pass in order to become apprenticed carpenters, plumbers, electricians, mechanics, and the like. Traditionally, working-class British and other European kids in their secondary schools left school at twelve or thirteen years of age without a formal education, prior to World War II; and even today in countries like Turkey, for example, children have been leaving school at eight years of age! So there is nothing very surprising about working-class kids not being formally educated, but it by no means follows that they are illiterate, because they can usually master some basic reading, writing, and arithmetic in their inferior schools.

By the time that Zuma became an adult, it is said that he had mastered the rudiments of reading and writing in Zulu and had already learned how to speak English. The story is that, from his English-speaking Indian and white playmates, he acquired a rudimentary knowledge of English, and from blacks he learned Zulu, before teaching himself thereafter.

For these very good reasons, President Zuma says that he does not regard himself as an uneducated person, only a self-taught one, not that his political and racist enemies in the white South African media today generally care to portray him as anything other than a tribal illiterate who reportedly cannot even write his own name!

Zuma has said of his experiences on Robben Island that it was thanks to night schools that he organized with and for others in the prison that he furthered his basic education as well as his political education. This could not have been easy for him, given that he had no education to speak of in the first place, but it is very much to his credit that he did so. After a while, it is said that he was allowed to do a correspondence course from behind bars and get his Junior Certificate to standard-6 level, which was quite an achievement for him. While a Junior Certificate may not sound like much to those in the Western world, it is an official certificate that is officially recognized, and one that is not without some value if you come from Zuma's lowly background (his mother cleaned people's houses, and his father was a policeman who died when Zuma was young). It was also in prison that Zuma was able to organize and participate in the aforesaid mutual-learning classes that provided for a kind of mixed-ability working men's adult education. Zuma reportedly had a passion for reading anthropology and Shakespeare, his favorite play being, as we have heard, *Macbeth*.

According to Zuma and those who remember him in prison, he had plenty of time for reading. The only things he lacked were educational certificates from school and a degree from a university. And when it came to clandestine political education behind bars, he claims that there was time for study groups, discussion groups, and one-hour lunchtime lectures, as well as weekend lectures, news analysis, and so on, with the prisoners grading each other in terms of their levels of understanding, with multi-cell political committees organized to this end.

If do-it-yourself learning of this kind really was an unofficial or occasionally official hallmark of Robben Island prison life, there was an unexpected upside here to counter the deeply degrading and depressing downside of all else, including the harsh conditions and hard labor already mentioned, as well as the woeful lack of decent or any other kind of food. There can be no doubt that an active prison culture of self-taught learning of this kind certainly shaped for the better the political education, knowledge, understanding, and leadership of a future ANC and its government when it came to power, and in the case of Jacob Zuma, it will have made up for many of his educational childhood deficiencies. With time for in-depth discussions among political activists about South African and world politics and the role of political organizations to that end, there was knowledge to be prized by those with their hearts set on a political solution to their racially unjust problems. Stolen time for analysis, articulation, and an exchange of ideas by the underground branch of the Robben Island ANC was not to be sneezed at.

Prisoners of different ages, sentences, and levels of importance within the ANC were treated differently behind bars, with, as already explained, those spending their time in single cells like Mandela having far less room in which to maneuver, and others like Zuma in the general section of the prison where they came under less scrutiny and control.

Obviously the single-cell prisoners had fewer educational and other opportunities, not that Mandela needed them, given that he was already a qualified lawyer. Govan Mbeki—President Thabo Mbeki's father—was another of the more important ANC leaders in a single cell (he reportedly spent twenty-three years in Robben Island).

In contrast to the single cells, the general sections were like military barracks with the usual dormitories rather than cells, and, as anybody who has served in the armed forces knows, there are barrack room lawyers in most dorms who are only occasionally visited by officers or sergeants. So there is much more scope for clandestine activities and discussions of all sorts, as we know from all those World War II films of British soldiers digging escape tunnels under the floorboards of their dormitory huts, under the noses of their Nazi officers (not that there was anywhere to which to escape at Robben Island, other than the shark-infested sea)!

In the prison's general section, where Zuma was apparently a popular figure and an organizer of soccer matches, it is said that fellow ANC prisoners who recognized Mandela never or rarely ever had the opportunity to interact with him, other than in the chain gangs breaking up rocks with their pickaxes.

Because many ANC leaders acquired an intellectual depth that they did not have previously, it stands to reason that they were better negotiators and organizers in consequence, and they had even learned the value of being more tolerant and patient, racially and otherwise—and also with each other!—having an obvious need to survive as best they could and having also been exposed to the influence of some seriously good philosophical as well as political thinkers, intellectuals, and qualified lawyers. These ANC leaders astonished the world with their racial tolerance, wise negotiations, and patient forgiveness when they got into government and led their people—demonstrating clearly that, against all expectations, they were indeed up to the task of responsible government—and credit is of course due to them for this. How else to explain the subsequent good and responsible conduct of these prisoners when they got out of jail and swiftly found themselves in positions of government, if not by reason of the intelligently transforming Robben Island *contemplative* experiences (like monks in a monastery)? How else did these prisoners become so capable, smart, and able to govern?

So, as we see from all this, Nelson Mandela's formative years did not begin and end in childhood or shortly thereafter, as these years generally do with so many of us. His adult formative years took over where the all-important childhood years left off, turning him into the giant political leader and world statesman that he became, and this no doubt has accounted for his amazing, multilayered leadership qualities and personality, the virtues of which multiplied throughout his life, as he went through the triple whammy of his formative years: from day school and boarding school to university and the legal profession; to political campaigning and freedom fighting; and then to jail for twenty-seven years of in-depth thinking and learning of yet another (but quite useful) kind.

Even so, his childhood formative years are not to be discounted, and it is certainly true that leadership was in his genes from the cradle, notably from his father who was a black tribal leader and counselor who advised and mentored his tribal people while at the same time advising his tribal king on how best to lead and make leadership decisions (there were a goodly number of little tribal kings in South Africa once upon a time). So Nelson Mandela grew up during the first five to seven years of his life—before going to his English missionary school at seven years of age—in this kind of atmosphere, observing his father's leadership, listening to his wise words, and getting his character molded in the process, no doubt. His tribal hut and his village community will presumably have been full of conversation of how best to lead this person but not that person, how to deal with and get the best or worst out of different people, and how to persuade the tribal king to do the right rather than the wrong thing.

While Nelson's father certainly was illiterate, he was a shrewd observer who cleverly learned by observation, and he would have known how to box clever and stay ahead of the game to make the right rather than the wrong political and social moves within his tribe and between his tribe and other tribes (although, as we shall see later on in this book, he did make one hotheaded wrong move that resulted in his and his family's undoing!).

For these reasons Nelson Mandela's childhood formative years are not to be underestimated when contemplating how it was that he became the very shrewd and great calculating leader that he certainly became—far greater than his father, of course—although, as I say, there was more to it than that, in all the other, very extraordinary, adult formative years that followed from one season to the next and the next. And on each and every occasion of yet another formative experience, he rose beyond the call of duty and gave his all.

For a man who had been relentlessly under the Nazi jackboot of his Dutch-Afrikaner white oppressors who tried to deny his leadership qualities and rob him of his rightful place at the table—this was one hell of an achievement that not only took great strength of character, but intellectual abilities and political cunning and character insights also. While we can certainly say that it was Nelson's birth in his Xhosa tribe and his upbringing there where his leadership qualities were first inherited and first took hold—before all his rebirths later on when he first put to the test his leadership genes when he came to power—it was also the way in which, later on, he proceeded to graduate, as it were, to all kinds of other, very different leadership roles, to each of which he adapted with astonishing versatility and an extraordinarily rounded and cool character.

Because his life was shaped and reshaped time and again, there was never any knowing what final shape it would take.

Yet the goodness and morality running through him at all times is what made the difference between him and most other African or world leaders that we can think of (we have thought of a goodly number thus far in these pages). With regard to other African leaders, for example, the point is well taken in comparison with Robert Mugabe in Zimbabwe! Ditto Idi Amin in Uganda and countless others who will be happily forgotten by history, but not Nelson Mandela, who will be remembered with great affection, respect, and admiration and rightly so.

The thing to remember about the segregation of apartheid— a good old word that is indeed typically Dutch—is that blacks had no votes and no rights in their own country and were forced at gunpoint to live and stay in racially prescribed and segregated areas. They were booted out of their homes if they were already in areas that were not prescribed for them, and they were not allowed to travel without special permission to any white areas, to have sex with or to marry whites (let alone socialize with them), to get properly educated like whites, to work with whites (unless working for them in subservient roles), or to attend white schools unless by special permission for some very rare and extraordinary reason. This, too, was all part of the agonizing history that Nelson Mandela and millions of blacks had to endure.

Under South African apartheid, blacks were brutally, ruthlessly, and tyrannically denied their basic human and civil rights with all the racial arrogance and religious self-righteousness of the Dutch Protestant Church that blessed apartheid while the rest of the world's religions condemned it.

While apartheid governments could not and did not prevent British Christian missionary schools and colleges from educating a handful of blacks who were lucky enough to get into those schools, they certainly could and did prevent the vast majority of blacks from getting educated, and they tried—albeit without success—to prevent blacks from speaking the global language of English, preferring them to speak the nonglobal language of Afrikaner-Dutch instead, so that oppressed blacks—Nelson Mandela included—would have no voice in the outside world.

South Africa's black Anglican Archbishop, Desmond Tutu, tells a touching story about having been standing in a Johannesburg street as a young man with his black mother—a humble cleaner and cook in a school for the blind—when a white man in priest's clothing passed them by and raised his hat, wishing Tutu's mother good day. By all accounts they could have fainted, because they had never seen a white man do such a thing before! Tutu says that he could not believe his eyes to see a white man greeting him and his working-class mother in this way. It was against this background and on behalf of such people that Nelson Mandela wanted his place at the white man's table to bring justice, humanity, and democracy to his people and to teach the whites a more civilized and less racist way of living, to teach them how to do the decent thing and recognize or otherwise to raise their hats to blacks—not too much to ask, one would have thought!

The white man in priest's clothing who astounded Desmond Tutu and his mother—in the Johannesburg slum of

Sophiatown—turned out to be the very civilized Archbishop Trevor Huddleston, an English priest from the English town of Bedford and from the public boarding school of Lancing College in Sussex by the sea and the University of Oxford. There was no way that this friendly priest could be from the Dutch Reform Church! The table at which Nelson Mandela wanted his place was not a racially tolerant and polite Trevor Huddleston table, out of England, but a stern-faced and racially hostile and rude Dutch-Afrikaner table, out of Holland, which was a very different matter.

While it is not possible to tell a great man's entire story in a single book, film, television program, or newspaper article—because there is always so much more to be told, and who has the time and the tenacity to read it all, listen to it all, or watch it all?—it certainly is possible to tell the essential things about him and his story, as I am attempting in this book and with a goodly number of unexpected other details besides. But whatever is told is never going to be the truth, the whole truth, and nothing but the truth, however truthfully or otherwise it may be told. Even the man in question cannot tell the whole of his own story himself; others cannot tell it about him either, not in a single production of any kind, because it would take volumes of books to tell it, and several films or television programs as well.

But at least the essentials can be told, essentials that are well worth knowing, and not least the essentials about Nelson Mandela's heart—a heart of gold to be sure. However a story is told about a man, if one cannot tell the story of his heart as well as his head—which in my experience is what matters most and what readers are usually most interested in—then forget it, because all else is superfluous and will very likely have been told previously elsewhere. What readers usually want to know most of all is what makes—or made—great men tick, and how can they know this if a writer does not deliver the heart and head of a great man to them on a plate (not literally, I hasten to add!)?

Where Nelson Mandela's head was concerned, it was as if he had found a way of remapping the brain of the interracial body politic (again, Gandhi never managed or even tried to do this), finding a new pathway to racial reconciliation, forgiveness, and harmony. This was a way that short-circuited all the other existing old pathways that were going nowhere fast because racially prejudiced and obstructive blood clots had gotten in the way for centuries to render the brain useless, or otherwise in need of a lobotomy!

Nelson Mandela has said that "a good head and a good heart are always formidable," and where his heart was concerned, he obviously could not have remapped the brain of the interracial body politic if that precious organ of his had not been in everything that he did, had not felt the urgent need for it, and had not had the strength of purpose for it.

What he achieved required a great deal of brain and a great deal of heart with which to *hearten* and *inspire* not only his own people, but also the world at large. And, for sure, Nelson Mandela was all heart.

His twenty-seven years behind bars, with all the soul-searching introspection and boxing clever that went with it, have clearly enabled him to get to know himself and tell himself (and also to tell others now) many well-considered truths. Yet if anything firmly and finally molded Nelson Mandela's character—so ironically for the better—it was perhaps this agonizing prison sentence more than everything else. It was perhaps this single agony that made for such a resolute and thoughtful, philosophical, and amazingly good-natured, chastened, and reflective person. While such a monumental agony would have destroyed or embittered many if not most others, it had the reverse effect on him, which really is *extraordinary*, is it not? This will have started in Nelson Mandela's Xhosa origins and during the first seven formative years of his childhood—which was a happy as well as a learning childhood of which he has said that he "was born free"—and ended with the nightmare of Robben Island in real character-developing style! Except to say that it did not end there—rather, it began!

Yet what had his Dutch-Afrikaner white oppressors tried to do with him before he became president?

They had tried, metaphorically speaking, to pluck out his literate tongue as they racially harassed, victimized, and discriminated against him, segregating him out of their lives and also his own life, treating him and all black others like lepers, and locking him up in jail with a view to throwing away the key when they failed to have him executed for treason, as most of them had hoped.

Long before his death, Nelson Mandela confessed "to being something of an Anglophile" in his autobiography, saying that when he thought of Western democracy and freedom, he "thought of the British parliamentary system."

Britain's former Prime Minister Tony Blair referred to Nelson's love of British culture on BBC Television at the time of the great man's death.

It is Britain's long-standing parliamentary system, the first of its kind in the world, that has delivered so many of the excellent reforms that a country requires in order to clean up its act nationally, socially, racially, and internationally; with the latter two reforms having a much better chance of following on from the former two, if the first two are honest enough to get it right in the first place and play fair in the first place.

Nelson Mandela said that the big difference between being up against the British, as opposed to the Dutch-Afrikaners, when campaigning for independence and racial equality, was that the British were more "farsighted" and "tolerant."

There were also many British anti-apartheid activists, intellectuals, liberal humanists, and non-racist others all campaigning in his favor in the UK, campaigning against the evil of apartheid.

And the reason why the British were so much more tolerant and farsighted was that they came from a more tolerant, farsighted, and socially and racially reforming culture that was very different from that of the Dutch-Afrikaners. They also came from a much wider, broad-brush world history, with all its insights and cross-cultural experiences that compensated for their other old colonial sins and racial shortcomings, not a narrow and parochial, blinkered Dutch-Afrikaner history. This was true of the British in South Africa and in other parts of the world where, unlike the Dutch-Afrikaners, the Brits were cleaning up their act that was indeed in need of cleaning up, giving back their colonies to their rightful owners (albeit not so rightful in South Africa!), and doing their best to make amends.

And all this, to cut a very long story short, is why Nelson Mandela and other black leaders much preferred the British to others—for their farsightedness and their tolerance, two qualities that the late Nelson Mandela had very much in common with the British.

CHAPTER THREE

In the High Bright Shadow of Nelson Mandela

WHEN THE CLOUD that was hanging over South Africa—with Nelson Mandela's last weeks and months—has cleared, it will soon be time for black South Africans to let in the sunshine again and not forget that their savior created an awful lot of sunshine for them during and after the dark days of apartheid (as we have seen already in the introduction and the first two chapters in this book and will continue to see in this chapter). Even from behind bars he radiated his never-say-die sunshine of hope and determination; and hope, as we know, is a hard plant to kill, as of course was the ever-hopeful Nelson Mandela, whose legacy will no doubt be a hard plant to kill.

Even during his darkest hours, detailed in the foregoing chapters, his sunshine smile kept shining triumphantly for millions of black South Africans he never knew or met in person, and from here on it is for them to keep smiling for his memory and for everything that he wanted for them; just as, in their time, the British, for example, kept smiling for their national icons (the aforesaid Winston Churchill and Lord Nelson) because it was in their history and blood to do so, and as the French, for example, have kept smiling for Napoleon, and the Catholic world has kept smiling for its popes. This is how most nations define themselves and believe in themselves—believe in the meaning and value of their history—and it is how South Africa can best define and believe in itself from here on, in the confidence that Nelson Mandela has given them much to smile about and that they must not allow anyone else to wipe that smile from their faces or the face of their country.

In particular, in this chapter, we look at the practical difference that Mandela's racial and political policies made to keep his people smiling. What good did the practical differences that Mandela made actually do, and in what way did his differences add value?

In short, Nelson added great value to the economy, self-belief, and good governance of his country, but at the continuing expense, alas, of the millions of unchanged South African poor.

Almost two decades later, this has become a burning issue that can make or break South Africa in future years.

Mandela has shown the way and also set the standard that the ANC leadership and the trade union leadership can uphold if they are of a mind to do so. He has set the tone and the example. As everybody knows, there is no way that the South African poor would have had any brighter hopes or prospects or better conditions or wages under their former white oppressors who were, of course, absolutely indifferent to their needs.

But it now falls to President Zuma and his government to do something seriously positive for the poor and needy and not ignore their plight, as other governments have done in their time in different parts of the world (India and Pakistan and so many other countries besides). South Africa's rock-bottom poor have continued to remain poor while the black African middle classes and upper classes have become rich beyond their wildest dreams (again, thanks to Nelson Mandela) and for the first time in their history, just as the whites have continued to get rich, as before, apart from those who have lost their jobs to blacks, or have left the country in disgust or despair because they don't like the lack of jobs for them, or the violence, or the equality with blacks in South Africa these days.

But the first thing to understand about Nelson Mandela's excellent and eminently sane black presence and moral leadership, when he first came to power, is the very big difference that it made when apartheid was finally abolished and then long overdue. The republic of black South Africa was founded some two decades ago in 1994, which is when the sun really shone for black South Africa and its multicolored rainbow nation. A new and dazzling class of black superstars suddenly emerged as an educated elite in political life, business, the arts, sports, and other professions, all of whom burst out of the darkness into the sunshine for the first time in their history.

With the ANC in charge of and under Nelson Mandela's presidency—as a single-party government and with a land-slide victory of black votes in its favor (a landslide victory that it still enjoys today under President Zuma)—there was abso-lutely nothing that this party and government could not have done, for good or ill; but under Mandela's influence it wisely acted for the good.

The difference that the ANC made for the good was not just racial, moral, and political, but also economical, material, and financial; and this was so very much for the better and it could otherwise have been lost to the worst of all possible outcomes if matters had not been in Mandela's very capable and safe hands. There almost certainly would have been inter-racial bloodshed and carnage on a vast scale, as the South African economy went down the pan, but it never happened, thanks to the smiles that Mandela put on most black and most surprised and relieved white faces equally (the brown-skinned Indian were not complaining either). There was of course the scary violence of the criminal underclass that turned to violent crime in order not to remain poor, but most white, Indian, and upper-class black Africans successfully ring-fence themselves against this (not all, but most).

With no opposition to speak of, there was virtually nothing that Nelson Mandela and his new ANC government could not have done. It could have given the white minority hell had it not declined to do so. It could have gloated and shown no gracious magnanimity whatsoever to whites in its electoral victory, which it also declined to do. On the contrary, it was amazingly gracious and considerate of white feelings and aspirations as, to everybody's surprise, it welcomed the continued participation of whites as Mandela's black Christians taught the whites of the Dutch Reform Church how to be good Christians for a change!

Mandela and the ANC could have stirred up racial hate against whites, which, again, it declined to do, as it went out of its way to avoid a racial bloodbath when many blacks might understandably have been (and very probably were) bitter and angry, full of racial hate, and calling for white men's blood. The ANC could have punished whites for their apartheid sins. There could have been a mass exodus of whites and foreign investors fleeing violence, similar to the mass exodus of Uganda Asians in the bad old days of Idi Amin. White properties and business premises could have been raided en masse and burnt to the ground. Whites could have been strung up and lynched (as blacks were strung up and lynched by whites and their Ku Klux Clan in the Southern states of America back in the 1950s and 1960s). But, happily, none of this happened (as the whites heaved a great sigh of relief).

What happened instead was that with all the cards in its hands—for the first time in South African history—the ANC turned the other cheek to whites in the best of Christian traditions, which is more than the old Dutch-Afrikaners had ever done to blacks when they had the upper hand and went out of their way to severely humiliate, persecute, and punish blacks. And it was this turning of the other cheek that made a very big economic difference indeed, and will continue to make a difference for as long as the other cheek is turned. If things go wrong in the South African economy now that Mandela is gone and has become past history—as things are already going wrong, in view of the world recession—it won't be because racially turning the other cheek did not work. Probably, now that South Africa's ailing economy is falling behind the rapidly expanding economies of its neighbors with their much higher growth rates, its best course is to invest in those economies until its own recovers.

Being mindful of what could be lost economically and financially, Nelson Mandela and South Africa's black leaders demonstrated that they were no fools where capitalism and foreign investment were concerned. They shrewdly collaborated with the multinational companies and banks instead of upsetting their apple cart, as a bloodbath or financial ineptitude or incompetence would most certainly have done, and also as the whites had predicted that the blacks would do, no doubt secretly hoping that this would be the case (with a view to their making a comeback if and when the ANC government fell on its face).

But under Nelson Mandela's wise guidance—and on his watch subsequently—nothing impractical or economically incompetent or damaging happened. On the contrary, he and the ANC turned out to be very pragmatic, as they and the economy went from strength to strength, and very racially forgiving indeed, albeit at the expense of neglecting the poor and needy as before, during the apartheid era. For ten years I have been visiting South Africa and seeing the excellent effects of all this (the astonishing upside, in addition to the distressing downside for the poor).

What happened was the introduction of racial reconciliation and forgiveness programs and confessional hearings, designed to forgive whites for their apartheid sins as soon as they confessed and repented them, and also designed to placate and compensate blacks with grievances against whites for the terrible injustices they had suffered. Whites were given the chance to make amends, as some did, while others did not, refusing to participate in these programs or to show up at their hearings. A great deal of ANC thought and wisdom had gone into all this, for which Nelson Mandela could take the chief part of the credit, if not all the credit, given that, as an adored founding-president, he could have done a Zimbabwean Robert Mugabe, for example, which he never did and never would have, being no despot or lunatic, and also being head and shoulders above leaders like Mugabe. Nor did he want to have the status of a saint bestowed upon him by the adoring millions. On the contrary, he reminded them that he was no saint, unless, as he wisecracked, the definition of a saint is a sinner who keeps trying!

His humor was sufficiently self-deprecatory and laden with witty understatement to endear him to the masses, demonstrating that he did not take himself or his godlike status too seriously, demonstrating that he could see the funny side of things, including himself, and did not lack a light or common touch. On account of his very special blend of humor, he was neither pompous nor arrogant, as so many national and world leaders are.

This was a triumphant, but delicate and precarious time in 1994, when the black victors' thoughts very naturally turned to putting the past right and correcting those responsible for its terrible wrongs—albeit not in a heavy-handed, spiteful, or counterproductive way, but in a subtle way. The ANC and its black leaders could not have been more gracious to the whites, but not in a way that compromised or demeaned the moral integrity, dignity, and standing of the blacks and their leaders who guided them, or of the black Christian churches that blessed them—churches in which there was no fanaticism as we have seen from Muslims, for example, in Africa and elsewhere when they want to revenge themselves upon on specific groups or, for that matter, as we have seen from the fanatical religion of the Protestant Dutch-Afrikaners in previous apartheid days.

No doubt the Dutch-Afrikaner whites—whose Dutch Reform and German Lutheran churches had condoned the apartheid wrongs that had been done to blacks—were thanking their lucky stars that Mandela and his followers were Christians and not Muslims! To this day, a majority of the black population worldwide is Christian—not the Zulu President Zuma and others like him, but certainly most others. Virtually every black man and woman I've met in South Africa is proud to be a Christian of one kind or another. Nelson Mandela was, as already observed, a Methodist, as was his old enemy Margaret Thatcher.

This was a very testing time in 1994, during which there was much to gain and also to lose, and the practical difference that was made by Nelson Mandela and the ANC was that what there was to lose did not get lost. On the contrary, it was made safe and secure as it increased in value. In short, the enormous practical differences that were made for the better were *political* (with policies that were much more acceptable, not just to South African blacks, but to South African whites and the outside world as well); *moral* (with a morality that was so much cleaner and better than the evils that had gone previously under apartheid's false cloak of spurious religious morality); *economic, business-related, and financial* (with sanctions lifted and foreign investors reassured that it would be business as it had been in the days before sanctions, resulting in the return of economic growth and new investors keen to increase that growth); *diplomatic* (with a new and credible statesmanship that was good for the country and its place in the world); and *interracial* within South Africa, with an end to racial friction and conflict and with the restoration of racial peace.

These were all very big practical differences that added much value to South Africa socially, racially, and economically, and were all feathers in Nelson Mandela's cap. This is why he has cast a high, bright shadow over his nation that not only persisted until the time of his death this year, but that will also remain in South Africa still, at least for the immediate future, and hopefully for the longer-term foreseeable future (depending on how far and for how long it is possible to foresee!). Apartheid's guilty white men—who had been chiefly those Dutch-Afrikaners and their predecessors whose sins and atrocities of which we shall be reminded in much more detail in this chapter—were not put in the stocks. They were encouraged to put their past behind them and work alongside the blacks for their own good as well as for the good of the country. It was all hands to the pump, and the new spirit of interracial goodwill that was on offer. Society did not become polarized or fragmented in Mandela's rainbow nation because he demonstrated very clearly that all races could and should pull together, that a racially divided country could come together and heal its wounds, and that this was what South Africa must continue to do now that Mandela is dead, of course.

Mandela's aforesaid autobiography—first published in London in 1994, four years after he was finally released in 1990 from his twenty-seven-year life imprisonment sentence—was all part of the high bright shadow that the great man was casting in the bookshops. Nelson had been busily writing his book secretly in jail and hiding it from the guards, and continuing as soon as he was released from jail in 1990 before taking up his presidential duties in 1994. He was also awarded his Nobel Peace Prize in 1993, so when he launched himself as the first black president of his country, he did so with a new book and his Nobel Prize. His credentials were indeed impeccable.

Patti Waldmeir of the *Financial Times* in London said that Nelson Mandela had given us "one of the most extraordinary political tales of the twentieth century" from which we could understand the "genesis of greatness," as indeed we could; while Sir David Steel of the British Liberal Party spoke of the extraordinary mixture of "courage, persistence, tolerance, and forgiveness" to be found in Nelson Mandela and his book (to which one could add, stubborn but bright idealism and optimism in a deeply and darkly cynical world).

As a former *Financial Times* journalist, I know perfectly well that most of the *Financial Times* readers and a goodly number of its journalists were expecting Nelson Mandela and the ANC to fall on its face in 1994 or shortly afterwards, and South African whites to hopefully come back to power again to save the economy! My last article for the *Financial Times* in February 1995, a year after Nelson Mandela and the ANC came to power and more than two decades after I had first worked for the paper, was in favor of promoting black graduates in British banking when only Britain's Midland Bank (subsequently sold to HSBC) was doing this (the other three major high-street clearing banks—Barclays, NatWest, and Lloyds—were doing no such thing).

My article was entitled "Recognising the Barriers"—the barriers of color prejudice and segregation against university-educated and other blacks in British banks—and it was the first to criticize Britain's major high-street banks (with the exception of Midland) for not having equal opportunities for black graduates and monitoring their progress within their financial institutions, some thirty years after Britain had its first race relations institute and antidiscrimination laws in the 1960s.

Britain had its first Indian member of Parliament, Dadabhai Naoroji, as early as 1892, followed by dozens more Asian and black immigrant members thereafter from the late nineteenth century and early twentieth century, right through to the present day, with the first two black members being Diane Abbott and Paul Boateng in 1987 (the latter of whom was at the aforesaid 2013 Royal Performance of the Mandela film in Leicester Square when Mandela's death was suddenly announced there after the film), all of which is worthy of note in this book because it testifies to the increasing racial tolerance and farsightedness of the racially, socially, and politically reforming British.

Britain has been way ahead of the other predominantly white nations of this world—not just at government level, but also at street level among the public, given that all these members of Parliament had to knock on people's front doors and get ordinary British and chiefly white people (once upon a time) to vote for them.

India's Dadabhai Naoroji in 1892 was soon to be followed by high-achieving Indians and Sikhs from all walks of life who settled in the United Kingdom for the next 121 years, the first and biggest group of immigrant members of Parliament (after the Jews) in the House of Commons (a sprinkling of others went into the House of Lords, as we shall see in chapter ten). Two other Indian members—a Conservative and a Communist—swiftly followed in Naoroji's footsteps before the 1947 Indian Independence Act.

So there really has been no color bar or institutional racism in British politics or the public at large in the United Kingdom, where there has been nothing to stop immigrants with colored skins and different religions from getting ahead if they were of a mind to do so (ditto Britain's Jews of course, who go back earlier in history). Naoroji was a Parsi Indian who was affectionately known as the Grand Old Man of India. The South African Dutch-Afrikaners and their ancestors in Holland can make no such long-standing historical claims to racial enlightenment or tolerance, of course. Holland did not receive or provide for its first black immigrants until the 1980s, and, during World War II, it did very little to resist Hitler, while it reportedly deported more Jews than any other European nation outside Nazi Germany, and more of its men than those of any other European nation volunteered to fight for the Nazis.

The *Financial Times* in London, for which I wrote my article, is Britain's and the world's foremost financial and economic daily newspaper, whose founder and owner once saved Winston Churchill from bankruptcy (but that's another story!). In the City of London, this paper is often referred to as "the pink un" because it is printed on pink paper, chiefly for business, financial, economic, and political readers concerned with keeping the British and other economies of the world "in the pink." While it has always been a capitalist right-wing paper, it has also given space to left-wing and other noncapitalist political views, as well as to third world and multiracial views, so we can see from this example that there has always been a strong body of moral and political support for blacks and Asians in the British media (with one or two notable exceptions!) where so many high-profile blacks and Asians are employed to this day, which is one of the reasons Nelson Mandela was pro-British and preferred to deal with Britain rather than the Dutch-Afrikaners.

The year before my *Financial Times* article, the late South African journalist, anti-apartheid campaigner, and *Cry Freedom* author (about which an excellent film has been made) Donald Woods told us in the *Sunday Times* that Nelson Mandela had "gone beyond mere consensus" and moved ahead of his followers and contemporaries to "break new ground" (as he certainly had), comparing Mandela to such great world leaders as President Lincoln (he who abolished slavery in the United States) and Mahatma Gandhi, who was chief among those who won independence from the British.

With common consent—unless you happened to be a die-hard Dutch-Afrikaner racially and politically biased against him—Nelson Mandela's was always the wise, kindly, and nonviolent voice of reason, racial reconciliation, and forgiveness for white people's racial sins in South Africa. Always the economically and financially shrewd voice, he made a great deal of sense to the *Financial Times*, which is why his book got its aforesaid rave review in that hard-nosed business newspaper.

It was Nelson Mandela who—having heinously suffered under apartheid, which had almost but not quite been the death of him (given his trial for treason for which the death penalty was in order)—told everybody to forgive, forget, and move on. As we might expect, this was easier said than done and a very big request indeed (as we shall see in chapter five). But Nelson asked it and got it and in this way managed to avert a bloodbath of revenge against whites by persuading blacks of the need if not to kiss and make up, then to forgive and forget, when he and his ANC party came to power. Miraculously, the blacks took Nelson's advice. Under his mighty influence and also the equally mighty influence of the incomparable Anglican Archbishop Desmond Tutu, they showed their former white oppressors how to behave in a civilized way, how they would have behaved if they had had any true morality about them.

The boy from tribal beginnings had made it, but what a terrible price he had to pay in order to make it. In Johannesburg, Mandela first lived in "Soweto," the name of which is an acronym for South Western Townships, where Mandela lived during his early life and marriage, in a small council/municipal house that was built of brick with a tin roof, a concrete floor, and a bedroom that was so small that the double bed took up most of the space! Go there and see it for yourself. But, for your personal safety, go with a trusted tour guide or black friend. There was an outside toilet and tiny garden in a very small plot of land that Mandela has described as "a postage stamp," like all the other plots of land that surrounded it. But it was better by far than the appalling shantytown hovels and slums that made up the greater part of Soweto. Mandela lived in West Orlando, which was the more respectable end of town, and one can visit his former home there to this day, as it has been turned into a museum, so one can see for oneself how cramped it was. It is just beyond the outskirts of Johannesburg.

Because of all the open fires in Soweto, there is a famous cloud of "Soweto mist" that hangs over the place most of the time, and it is very instructive indeed to visit the unhygienic shantytown hovels there and talk to the desperately poor inhabitants who live in these filthy threadbare dwellings in which they can hardly move (but do remember to tip them very handsomely indeed if you have a conscience). I met a massively smiling young man there, with perfect English, who asked me to give his regards to the Queen of England! And when I told him that I would do so because I had tea with her at Buckingham Palace regularly, he went into hoots of laughter. I added that she was very disappointed if I could not make it and that she was not amused if I turned up late.

Many people have a good sense of humor in Soweto and South Africa generally, where there is little to smile about in the former township, and there is also a good soccer team and stadium there, as well as a good jazz club, an ensemble of violinists, church choirs, and some magnificently brightly colored murals. Here is a place where the locals are desperately doing their best not to let their slum land—and their violent gangland criminals—get them down, as they keep their chins decidedly up. They deserve better, very much better. They also have vigilantes who protect inhabitants from the local gangsters and rapists with whom they deal personally, rather than calling the police and waiting for them to turn up.

What else can I tell you about this gutsy, inspirational, and potentially heartbreaking place? If you go there to see for yourself, you will not be disappointed. Soweto is generally regarded as the soul of black South Africa and the Harlem of Johannesburg for its people, its history, its uprising, and its unique position in black African consciousness. But, let me repeat, don't go alone. Take a minder or go on a protected tour. Go there and discover what apartheid was really like at its lowest level and how the harsh and ugly reality of life remains with it to this day. Go to the aforesaid Apartheid Museum in Soweto.

To Dutch-Afrikaner whites, apartheid was just an empty word that lightly and carelessly tripped off the tongue, because it had no ill effects on them. It was a cozy little self-righteous word to verify their presumed racial superiority that demanded that they were born separate from and way above such wretched places and people on whom they could wipe their feet any day of the week, not that they ever went anywhere near such places as Soweto unless they had to. But to those who were cruelly oppressed and persecuted by the sledgehammer of apartheid and condemned to live in filthy places like Soweto and all other such shantytowns, it was a word full of misery and despair that invoked their obviously understandable resentment and hate.

Why should a young, newly married black lawyer like Nelson Mandela have been forced to live in such a place as Soweto, even in the respectable and cleaner end of town? Why should any blacks have been forced to live in such a festering place after their homeland had been stolen from them, the likes of which could be and still are found all over South Africa to this day, like running sores on the landscape? How bad was apartheid, and what did it entail? We have touched on this in the previous chapter, and we return to it again now with some more detail.

Nelson had been falsely accused and found guilty of having tried to organize a revolution to overthrow the Afrikaner apartheid governments, which he had not done.

He and his ANC colleagues had organized a national defiance campaign of protest and civil disobedience against apartheid, and they had nonviolently sabotaged some telephone and rail lines, power plants, and army depots in locations. They had specifically targeted places where there were no people who could come to grief. But he and his fellow black activists were brought to court for all that, with a view to having them executed. Instead of execution, they got life imprisonment, not least because the outside world was up in arms about their phony trial, along with everything else where they were concerned.

Life imprisonment for nonviolent acts of sabotage at locations where there was no targeting of civilians or threat to human life! This was perverse justice that was disproportionate to the crime (acts of sabotage intended as a bargaining tool to bring these whites to the table that they were avoiding like the plague!). To give Nelson and his colleagues life imprisonment was like taking a sledgehammer to a nut. But that's what apartheid did. It cracked nuts with a sledgehammer in its physically and psychologically bullying way. But it did not crack the nut—or indeed harden the heart of—Nelson Mandela, who smiled sweetly and carried on smiling sweetly for twenty-seven years! The Dutch-Afrikaners during those apartheid years were some of the biggest physical and psychological bullies known to recent history.

One cannot say that Nelson Mandela was "not a proper man" in any of this, not being more violent in his reaction to apartheid. Let's not forget that we are talking here about one who had been a boxer in his spare time in order to relieve the tensions of his life at the end of a hard day's work. As he has explained in his autobiography, he went to a community gym in Johannesburg where he worked out and sparred with a black professional boxer, in order to "lose" himself and no doubt a significant amount of stress and anger in something that was not part of the interracial struggle. He found the rigorous exercise to be a welcome outlet for all the pressures that he was under, and it left him feeling "refreshed" and strong for the next round against his apartheid oppressors, who broke all the rules and did not believe in referees or indeed Queensbury rules, as they played dirty. By his own admission, he was "never an outstanding boxer," but he was good enough to stand his ground in the boxing ring as well as outside of it; an unlikely boxer for a lawyer or indeed a president of South Africa, this former schoolboy stick-fighting champion from a black Xhosa tribe.

When Nelson Mandela and the ANC were obliged to turn to acts of nonviolent sabotage, the Afrikaner whites had rejected every other means suggested or enacted of resolving their differences with him—discussions, dispatches, deputations, marches, strikes, voluntary imprisonment, consultations, negotiations, representations, and so on. So they left the ANC and its black activists no choice but to turn to sabotage as a last resort (the very thought of sitting around a table with black Africans and having to breathe the same air as them in order to bargain with them was anathema to these Dutch-Afrikaners!). As Mandela said in his autobiography, "it is the oppressor who defines the nature of the struggle," leaving the oppressed with no choice but to mirror what is being done to them and to "fight fire with fire."

This all seems mind-bogglingly stupid and crass now, but that's how things were back then, as long as sixty-five years ago in 1948 and the years that followed, and as short as a mere two decades ago in 1994 when the thaw began to set in at last and Nelson Mandela and the ANC first came to power to found the Republic of South Africa.

The following are the timelines of these events and also of those for Nelson Mandela personally:

- 1918—Nelson Mandela was born in the Eastern Cape
- 1941—Ran away from an arranged marriage at twenty-three
- 1943—Joined the ANC, enrolled for a law degree, and later cofounded the ANC Youth League
- 1944—Married his first wife, Evelyn Mase, who gave him four children
- 1952—Qualified as a lawyer and formed his own law firm
- 1956—Was charged with high treason with 155 other activists, but the charges were dropped after a four-year trial
- 1958—Divorced his first wife and married his second wife, Winnie
- 1960—Went underground when apartheid was outlawed; sixty-nine black protestors were shot dead in the Sharpeville Massacre
- 1962—Was arrested and given five years behind bars for sabotage
- 1964—Was charged yet again and sentenced to life imprisonment
- 1968—His mother and son died; he was not allowed to attend their funerals
- 1964—Behind bars on Robben Island for eighteen years where he contracted tuberculosis
- 1982—Arrives in Pollsmoor Prison on the mainland
- 1988—Seventy-two thousand people at Wembley Stadium in London sang "Free Nelson Mandela," which was televised to millions around the world
- 1990—Was freed from prison when the ANC became legal again

- 1992—Divorced his second wife, Winnie
- 1993—Won his Nobel Peace Prize
- 1994—Was elected South Africa's first black president
- 1998—Married his third wife, Graça Machel, who was formerly married to the president of Mozambique
- 1999—Stepped down as president
- 2001—Was diagnosed with prostate cancer
- 2004—Retired from public life at eighty-five years of age for "quiet reflection"
- 2005—His son died of AIDS
- 2010—Appeared at the closing ceremony of the World Cup
- 2011—Went into a Johannesburg hospital for health tests
- 2012—Was hospitalized again for a long-standing abdominal complaint

What a sorry tale of needless woe the above is, reflecting man's racist inhumanity to man. All Nelson Mandela ever wanted to do was, as he said in court, to "cherish the ideal of a democratic and free society in which all persons live together in harmony and with equal opportunities. It is an ideal which I hope to live for and to achieve. But if needs be, it is an ideal for which I am prepared to die." But there's more yet, as follows, by way of a fuller explanation and historical perspective to these events.

1948: Dutch-Afrikaners got their independence from the British and imposed a massive legislative apartheid, like a suffocating wet blanket over South Africa's people, in virtually every walk of life, under which Nelson Mandela and the black ANC party were eventually banned and their existence and arguments thereby denied. This was "a crazy concept born of prejudice and fear," according to Field Marshal Smuts, a previous Dutch-Afrikaner prime minister of South Africa in the days of the British.

1949: The Dutch-Afrikaners swiftly introduced their Prohibition of Mixed Marriages Act, soon followed by the so-called Immorality Act, both of which made sexual relations and marriages between whites and nonwhites illegal, would you believe? Then, later on, came their Population and Restriction Act, identifying all South Africans by race and segregating them into different ghettoes, outside of which they were not allowed to live or hang out! These acts were the absolute essence of apartheid, so was it any wonder that there was defiance, civil disobedience, and eventually acts of sabotage from Nelson Mandela and others in response to these tactics by the Dutch Afrikaners with the blessing of their Dutch Reformed Church and German Lutheran churches? Any nonwhites not carrying their identity cards with them at all times could be, and often were, tried in court, fined, or imprisoned for this minor offence; and let us repeat that this was all done with the blessing of the Dutch Reformed Church! As Nelson Mandela has said, "the Dutch Reformed Church supported apartheid and [also] the [German] Lutheran Mission," while all the other Christian churches were actively opposed to it. If left to Dutch and German Christians, apartheid would have reigned supreme in the eyes of their God in South Africa, where the Dutch Reformed Church was, Nelson told us, "the faith of nearly all the Afrikaner people" with whom this church walked "hand in hand," as it suggested to its converts that they were "God's chosen people," while the "blacks were a subservient people" in a country that "should be a white man's country forever." As we also see, the Dutch and the German settlers also walked hand in hand in South Africa. They did not walk hand in hand with Brits or too many others. This was a Dutch-German game.

1952: Nelson Mandela and Oliver Tambo opened South Africa's first black law firm on Johannesburg's Fox Street, where they were joint senior partners in their own legal practice, but were not infrequently treated with contempt and hostility when they appeared in court on behalf of their black clients—not just by white judges, but also by whites and policemen whom they were trying. One Dutch-Afrikaner judge refused to have Nelson Mandela in his court unless and until he produced his law degree for his inspection!

1976: Fifteen thousand black schoolchildren in Soweto protested against the apartheid government's new ruling that half of all classes must be taught in Afrikaans rather than English in the future, even though schoolchildren and their teachers did not want to learn or teach the language of their oppressors. When protests got underway, the white police opened fire without warning and killed many children, including thirteen-year-old Hector Pieterson. When the children (and presumably others) fought back with sticks and stones, two white men were stoned to death, and hundreds of children were wounded. Nationwide riots by adults were triggered by this children's riot in Soweto, which, as already mentioned in this chapter, became the very soul of black Africa in consequence.

1977: Nelson Mandela's home was raided by Dutch-Afrikaner police while he was behind bars, and his wife, family, and furniture were all transported to a different location some 250 miles away to be segregated once again, where they and their furniture were dumped in front of a tin-roofed shack with no heating, lighting, toilet, or water, in an area where white farmers ruled the roost over poor blacks.

1977: Black activist Steve Biko (whose slogan was "Black is Beautiful") was tortured and beaten to death by the Dutch-Afrikaner police for twenty-two hours after being stripped naked and manacled by them.

1984: Twenty years after Nelson Mandela was put behind bars for life, Bishop Desmond Tutu was awarded a Nobel Peace Prize for using his religious influence to bring about peace between whites and nonwhites, notwithstanding all the many sins of the white man.

1990: Nelson Mandela and the other ANC activists who had been given life imprisonment were finally released from jail, triggering the abolition of apartheid, in consequence of the increasingly harmful economic sanctions and political isolation put upon the white apartheid governments of South Africa by the outside world. For sure, life imprisonment of Nelson Mandela and his colleagues had been a carefully calculated and racially pernicious miscarriage of justice because it wasn't the apartheid government they had tried to overthrow. It was the ability to vote and a share in the government that they rightfully wanted and to which they felt their people were entitled. History soon proved this when they came to power, allowing white political parties and movements to this day, including white racist factions that still stick to their despicable old ways.

1993: Nelson Mandela and the Dutch-Afrikaner president, Frederik Willem de Klerk, were awarded the Nobel Peace Prize for finally bringing peace to South Africa by abolishing apartheid, which is when Nelson Mandela said, "We stand here today as nothing more than a representative of the millions of people who dared to rise up against a social system whose very essence is war, violence, racism, oppression, recession, and the impoverishment of an entire race of people." As it happened, de Klerk had color in his blood and his family tree from way, way back—Indian on one side and Hottentot on the other—in addition to his much more obvious French Huguenot and Dutch-Afrikaner blood.

2013: Nelson Mandela died nineteen years later—before his government reached its twenty-first birthday—at ninety-five years of age, having had six children, three of whom (two boys and a girl) died prematurely. But he died, by all accounts, a cheerfully contented and happy man after all he had been through, at one with and at peace with himself. He died, let us repeat, full of self-deprecating humor, charm, and magnificently memorable charisma, with a complete and philosophical lack of bitterness for the harsh treatment and racist injustices dished out to him over the years. He also died with an amazingly high and global (ambassadorial) profile, with an appeal that had been second to none in the world.

With a monumentally staggering life story such as his, with all its ups and downs, how can Nelson Mandela not have had global appeal, given that most people love a monumentally staggering life story? Who doesn't love the astounding and astonishing true stories of Winston Churchill, Mahatma Gandhi (Churchill's old enemy!), Napoleon Bonaparte, Lord Nelson, Alexander the Great, and so on? Mandela's outstanding example may continue to set the moral and political tone for a long time to come. His has been on a seventy-year journey since 1943, when he first joined the ANC.

In 1943, Britain was at war with Nazi Germany and was cheered on by many of South Africa's white Dutch-Afrikaners who physically attacked those British and fellow white Afrikaners in the streets who had joined the British Army to fight for the freedom and democracy in which die-hard Dutch-Afrikaners did not believe, identifying their fellow whites by word of mouth or their uniforms in order to target them.

In 1918, when Nelson Mandela was born, World War I was coming to an end, and the defeated Germans were signing an armistice with Britain and its allies, while the German king Kaiser Wilhelm was abdicating and fleeing to his friendly Dutch neighbors for refuge. Throughout the white man's history of South Africa, there has never been any love lost between the Dutch-Afrikaners and the British, not since two world wars, and so many other colonial contests and conflicts before that. While the Dutch-Afrikaners in South Africa today are polite enough to one and all, including the Brits of course, there are still plenty among them who don't like the Brits and will not forgive them for their history in South Africa, firstly for depriving the Dutch settlers (who got there first) of their power there, and secondly for morally and politically supporting the blacks from a distance after the Brits had left South Africa. So this is still a country in which there are racial undercurrents and tensions all around, between whites as well as between blacks and whites, and that's even before one gets to finding out where the Indians stand with regards to Brits and Dutch! They called the Brits "nigger lovers" for supporting the blacks. But consider this: all white men appear to have originally come out of South Africa, eighty thousand years ago, out of their caves—not black men, but white men. There was an exhibition at the British Museum in London in 2013 referencing this, demonstrating how the world's first whites came from South Africa and lived in the European Ice Age forty thousand years ago, after they left South Africa behind them, on an infinitely greater and longer than long Voortrek than that of the Dutch-Voortrekkers (more about them later this chapter)!

Breathtaking historical perspectives are shifting massively—awesomely—all the time, given that we have knowledge of them, as most of us don't (we do if we get our heads into books, attend the public exhibitions that tell us all about them, or watch television documentaries, but, unsurprisingly, the Dutch-Voortrekkers back then had a different historical and racial perspective, not least because they did none of these things, just as their descendants today do none or few of these things!). They thought that they had been "implanted by God" in the black man's land of the heathen on a religious mission (well, that was their excuse!).

But will Nelson Mandela and his influence live on and cheerfully haunt us for the better for a long time to come? Will others in South Africa and Africa be able to match him?

This remains to be seen—in this book and in real life—if the spirit of Mandela will live on. We have seen no comparable others, as yet, but let's not forget it is early days in the fledgling history of the Republic of South Africa. On the other hand, if we remember that when things are tough, it is usually the tough and supremely principled who get going, maybe those trying times of the 1940s and 1950s bred some tougher and more principled people than those being bred today, when things are not tough anymore for the educated black middle classes and the political leaders who are coming out of them.

As we can see from the foregoing timelines from 1948 to 1994 when the ANC came to power, forty-six years is a long time for a black race and its political party to stoically perserve, suffer, and make sacrifices in order to get its just rights and inherit its own country. Children are born and grow up and have children of their own in forty-six years, and some of them live and die. Life goes out of the window in forty-six years (Nelson Mandela touched his wife's hand not more than once during his twenty-seven years behind bars; how bruising and punishing was that?). Forty-six years was such a very long and outrageously disgraceful time for South Africa's blacks to have to wait for the racial justice and freedom that was being denied them. But they needed a savior, and along came Nelson Mandela, among others, but towering above all others. Cometh the hour, cometh the man.

But what would those men have done otherwise, without their hour in history? Nelson Mandela would probably have been a civil servant, since this was his first and only ambition until he became politicized. But what to make of it all if you are a reader outside South Africa today? What to make of it all both then and now? What to make of the other South

African black leaders who are not at all out of the same mold as Nelson Mandela?

And what to make of the illiterate and deeply impoverished lost souls who are in search of an urgently needed new deal in South Africa?

Nobody in their right mind would stray into the no-go areas of such lost and dangerous people, because a great many are not only violent, but also drugged and therefore half-crazed out of the misery of their minds. They live in communities in which they think nothing of killing each other, including burning their black enemies to death by putting rubber tires round their necks and setting fire to them! This is called "necklacing" and plenty of people get necklaced.

But the story of their criminal violence doesn't end there, because they come looking for whites and Indians in the upmarket neighborhoods where they live, shop, and socialize in order to mug them or break into their homes, schools, restaurants, or shops, not just after dark, but also in daylight. For this reason many of the white and Indian neighborhoods are necessarily ring-fenced.

This really is where the Dutch-Afrikaners come into their own! They certainly know how to defend and ring-fence themselves. They have been doing it throughout their long history, in one way or another, and they do it better than most. One is reassured behind their physical barriers, but not behind the barriers of their minds. But is it possible to have one without the other?

This ring-fencing is in evidence in most parts of South Africa where I have been traveling for the last decade—Chatsworth, Phoenix, Laudium, Claudius (all are Indian neighborhoods), Durban, Johannesburg, Soweto, Sandton City, Pretoria, Cape

Town, Stellenbosch, and Franschhoek, among others—where the only relatively safe areas are those that are suitably segregated or ring-fenced in one way or another, or otherwise protected by security guards!

In Pretoria, there is the aforementioned mighty Voortrekker Monument to visit, marking the Great Trek or People's Trek—mentioned earlier in this chapter—of some twelve to fourteen thousand Dutch-Afrikaner Boer farmers and their friends who marched inland from Cape Town for thousands of miles between 1835 and 1840. They did so in order to escape British domination and to seek new pastures, as well as to establish their military supremacy for a while—with their technologically advanced German machine guns, they established their supremacy over the Xhosa black tribes with their spears.

With these technologically advanced machine guns, they even established their supremacy over the British for a brief while, but only for a while, despite managing to kill more Brits than Brits killed them, again thanks to their superior German arms. But when it came to hand-to-hand and other forms of fighting in which German machine guns were absent, the odds were fairly even, until the Dutch-Afrikaners finally cracked when the Brits threw an excess of men into the battle like handfuls of sand against a window pane in the deadly machine gun fire. So the Brits got through in the end, albeit with greater loss of life.

But their Voortrekker "wagons westward" migration and cowboy "Wild West" mentality established Dutch-Afrikaner nationhood with two separate states, independent from the British—the Orange Free State and the Transvaal—that were recognized by the British.

The Voortrekker Monument is the place that the Dutch and all Dutch-Afrikaners like to visit most. They generally have no interest in most places of black, Indian, or British interest in South Africa today.

There are many white Dutch and other Afrikaners who have never visited the aforesaid black township of Soweto, the Apartheid Museum, Nelson Mandela's former home and museum, or the Robben Island prison off the coast of Cape Town where Nelson Mandela and other anti-apartheid activists were locked up for so long—they have never been on an homage to see these places for themselves, nor been to black churches to pray with black Christians.

They have never been to Mahatma Gandhi's settlement at Phoenix near Durban, to shop for Indian foods at Laudium near Johannesburg, to shop in Durban's very first Indian market in the center of that city (Victoria Market), or to visit the Hare Krishna temple at Chatsworth near Durban. For them, apartheid lives on, in their heads at least.

Interestingly, Dutch-Afrikaner South Africa, with all its neo-Nazi white prejudice against blacks and Indians, has not deterred Jews from settling and staying there, either when they fled from Hitler's Germany or later on. While the more liberal-minded and non-racist Jews, who helped Nelson Mandela in his anti-apartheid and freedom-fighting days, left for Britain, many right-wing and Zionist others have happily stayed on regardless of the racial prejudice there that at least has not been open (although I have met Dutch-Afrikaners who have told me privately that they regard the Jews as a "condemned race" for having killed Jesus Christ unless and until they repent!).

In my experience, Afrikaner society is very closed and will tell you that South Africa's antisocial or criminal classes will kill you—which is true—for your cell phone, camera, or car if you don't get out of it at a traffic light and hand over the keys when they put a revolver to your head! Not that this is any reason not to visit all the foregoing nonwhite places of interest that I have mentioned, given that one takes security precautions along the way, as many visitors from abroad do, including tourists, some of whom probably see more of these places than the Dutch-Afrikaners and other whites who live in South Africa today.

Instead of hailing a cab on the street—or risking public transport in all-black mini buses and on certain train routes—one can travel with black taxi drivers who are under contract and carefully vetted. Therefore, they will look out for you, as they are only too pleased to do, and one can make sure not to stop in a hired or other car at traffic lights. One can go on carefully guided and protected tours or simply remember not to take all manner of known risks.

The criminal and violent blacks who are a threat to whites, browns, and blacks equally are indeed potentially scary; they are the ones who are still in search of their lost souls and some home comforts and food, two decades after the foundation of Nelson Mandela's rainbow nation, but at least Zuma's ANC has declared that it is trying to do something about them. Some of these social rejects are organized into criminal gangs whose leaders profit, Fagin-like, from the rich rewards that their underlings bring, while others are freelance operators. A great many are infected with HIV or are on drugs that they also steal by breaking into doctors' surgeries, hospitals, and pharmacies, or anywhere else. Even one of Nelson Mandela's sons died of AIDS, while another, as we have heard, died in a car crash. So Nelson's has been a tragic family not just on account of its political past.

It really is important to get a clear idea of the two very different kinds of blacks that we are talking about in South Africa today—the brainy, educated, sophisticated, and civilized, and the others who are not so (how could they possibly be?)—with the former being wise enough to understand that they do need their professional white and Indian communities still, for business and investment purposes, and for all the other purposes that they need their professional classes, not to mention the sheer joy of interracial relationships between blacks, whites, and browns.

We have heard what a wise counselor and adviser to his tribal king that Nelson Mandela's illiterate father was, but he made one big and very unwise mistake when he snubbed a British magistrate in the days of the British Empire who had summoned him to his office to account for himself in a dispute with a herdsman over a stray ox! The herdsman had registered a complaint against Nelson's father that was being investigated by the British magistrate in the interests of justice regardless of rank and race, but Nelson's father stubbornly refused to answer the summons on the grounds that he was answerable to his Xhosa king, not an interfering and impertinent British magistrate!

However, given that his father's position had to be ratified by the magistrate, this resulted in his downfall when the ratification of his position in the House of Thembu was consequently withdrawn, so his family suddenly found itself in much reduced circumstances with a big question mark over its future. Nelson's father became stubborn on a matter of principle—that it was racially and morally wrong for a white British magistrate to have power over a black man in his own country with tribal allegiances to his own race and tribe—an example of where Nelson got his stubborn character from, as well as his racial dignity, independence, idealism, defiance, and resistance.

So, as already suggested, in these two essential, absolutely key respects, Nelson Mandela was very much like his father—a born leader, negotiator, and statesmanlike diplomat, but a man of massive and stubborn principle in the bargain, not to mention strength of obstinate purpose, even to his own detriment. This was in his blood and his nature very probably from the cradle, if you believe in nature more than nurture (not that Nelson wasn't nurtured that way as well). But it was from his black Christian mother from whom his religion and English-speaking education came, and this was just as important, if not more so, because without an education he would hardly have been noticed. As the only one of Mandela's father's wives who was a Christian, Mandela's mother introduced her son to Christianity, from which he got into the aforementioned Methodist school to become the first of his family to become educated. He went from strength to strength in different Wesleyan Methodist schools en route to becoming a lawyer, instead of remaining a tribal counselor perhaps, like his father before him, or even as—perish the thought—champion stick-fighter or boxer that, as we have seen, were two other skills of his!

When, in 1948, the Dutch-Afrikaner National Party of South Africa introduced blanket apartheid after it got its independence from the British—who, as we have heard, had not practiced such outrageous, heavy-handed, or institutionalized apartheid previously—the screws were really on Nelson Mandela and the ANC. On the contrary, the British, as we have already seen, had educated blacks in their missionary schools, while the Dutch-Afrikaner Hendrik Verwoerd (Minister of Native Affairs) had asked, "What is the use of teaching Bantu children mathematics when it cannot be used?" This was in a country in which ten times more was being spent on education for whites than for blacks. Nor did the British introduce legislation or a police state for a rigid and shameless system of apartheid at all levels and in virtually all sectors of society and workplaces.

The British did not drive six hundred thousand blacks from their homes—forcibly evicting them with armed police—and dump them in faraway fields where they had no choice but to live in wooden or tin shacks in the blistering heat without clean water and sanitation. They did not ban racially mixed marriages and relationships, as the Dutch-Afrikaners did in 1949 and 1950, or regularly raid their homes for evidence of interracial sex to be used in criminal prosecutions against consenting adults. The British, in the late 1940s and 1950s, were giving up their empire, not building it up, and learning from their mistakes, unlike the Dutch-Afrikaners. The British—who were not Dutch or Afrikaner Calvinists—did not twist their biblical scriptures in order to pretend that racial equality was against the will of God who had called for racial "diversification." On the contrary, as we know, many British churches, clergy, and bishops spoke out loudly against South African apartheid and have welcomed black and Asian priests.

Notwithstanding their strict religious morality and professed racial superiority, some of the white Afrikaners' top families and leaders will have had black blood in their own veins, about which they kept quiet! These distant veins stretching back like the roots of trees into colonial and racial history were a well-kept secret, including, it is claimed, the veins of Andries Pretorius, who led the aforesaid Dutch Voortrek (Great Trek) into the South African hinterland and heartland from Cape Town, after he had descended from East Indian slave grandmothers on both sides of his family.

When van Riebeeck, the founding father of white Afrikaner South Africa, turned up in 1653, he opened the doors to Dutch, Scandinavians, Germans, and, before long, Protestant French Huguenots on the run from Catholics in their own country. Many in these nationalities were or became very religious Protestant Calvinists. He also imported slaves from Indonesia and the island of Madagascar off the African coastline in the Indian Ocean; inevitably, they interbred with Dutch whites and gave rise to a so-called "colored" mixed race. So, as we see, not everybody wanted apartness, or if they did, they did not want to own up to it. That latter was generally the case.

Riebeeck's early Dutch settlers were religious zealots who not only wanted racial apartness in somebody else's country—apartness from the blacks that they found there and ruled with an iron fist—but from the greater European Christian religion as well, given that most of them really were strict and severe Calvinists, living literally by the imagined rule and word of God in their minds that were fed by their scriptures.

John Calvin, the French Protestant inventor of their puritanical and very simplistic religion, escaped to Geneva in Switzerland to preach his new scriptures from there, where they spread to Holland, some parts of Germany, and several parts of Scotland. Calvinism was and remains a very narrow and lopsided religion that was and is not a natural running mate with the more flexible Catholic Church, or indeed the more broad-minded and liberal-minded Anglican and other churches of the Church of England There is ample evidence to show that Calvin was anti-Semitic. In fact, one might reasonably argue that his was a religion that was tailor-made for apartheid (the Dutch Protestant Church, to which most of the Dutch-Afrikaners belonged, and to which many of their sons and daughters belong to this day, is a narrow and purely Calvinist church).

This, to cut a long story short, is the kind of long-term and short-term history that the black Christian Methodist Nelson Mandela and his ANC colleagues were up against centuries later, when he became the president of the ANC in 1994. It was Mandela's declared mission to mentally and intellectually cleanse South Africa of its white apartheid mentality, speaking as a Methodist, of course. And he spoke out against it and saved some or many of the Dutch-Afrikaners from themselves in the fullness of time, including South African blacks and the national economy, with the exception, as always, of course, of the black underclass that we have already said is the next big challenge.

It is a challenge that will never go away and one that has been returning with a vengeance even while Nelson Mandela was dying at the end of his life. We shall return to this subject in chapter five when President Jacob Zuma—South Africa's current president—enters our story, he who has taken the baton from his predecessors and must run with it now and see how well he can match them, including the mighty Mandela, of course (he who started it all!). Zuma was in regular attendance with the Mandela family as the great man's life came to a close, and he kept South Africa and the outside world regularly informed of Mandela's declining health. He showed his respects along with everybody else who mourned for Mandela.

But one last word about Mandela and South Africa's extremely poor black millions—in the following chapter—before we move on to what President Zuma can possibly do about them and for them.

We have seen in this chapter the very real difference that Nelson Mandela made to keeping the racial equality and capitalist show on the road when he first came to power, and the very real difference that this made to the economic as well as the moral cause of black and white South Africa equally almost twenty years ago. We have seen how he really did practice what he preached with regard to forgiving the former white apartheid oppressors and persecutors of South African blacks and other races as well as South Africa's money with regard to the economy and jobs. He kept the foreign investments, goodwill, and harmony flowing by taking great care not to upset the capitalist apple cart without which there would almost certainly have been nothing but bloodshed, carnage, and economic collapse, leaving South Africa immeasurably worse off.

He was not only a good Christian but a good businessman as well, and he achieved all this that has lasted for the greater part of two decades. It is very possible that only he could have done it. But in order to do this, he put the problems of South Africa's extremely poor millions of unemployed and poorly paid on the back burner, as did his successors, as we shall see in the following chapter, before arriving at President Zuma in the chapter after that.

CHAPTER FOUR

Nelson Mandela's *Miserables*

WE HAVE NOW seen, in the first three chapters, how it was that Nelson Mandela was the real deal, but not, alas, for the millions of South Africa's unemployed and extremely poor. Given the limited hand of cards that Lady Fortune had dealt to Mandela, we can also see that he knew how to play his cards to the best advantage in more ways than one on a needs basis, and that he knew what his priorities were.

First came his moral leadership, the avoidance of a bloodbath, the resultant economic and foreign investment success in the absence of a bloodbath, and then came the turning of a very superior freedom movement into a successful government.

But his freedom movement has turned out to be like no other because, for two decades now, it has been gradually turning itself into a proper government, rather than the mere freedom movement that it was, and it is currently maturing as such. The reason why he managed to achieve such a superior freedom movement is because he converted the ANC and other black South Africans to his amazing culture of patient compromise—a rare thing in Africa to be sure—to go with his moral superiority and business leadership already discussed in this book.

The ANC is, as it always has been, a very different and infinitely better kind of freedom movement from the bottom up, which is why it is currently able to be successfully converting itself, slowly but surely, into a proper government that is—thus far and fingers crossed!—no longer merely a freedom movement as before, which is more than other freedom movements have succeeded in doing. They have either fallen apart or turned themselves into tyrannical dictatorships in order not to fall apart.

In case anyone doubts that the freedom movement that he bequeathed was in any way extraordinary or superior to others, just look at the others in question. One does not need to be a professor, graduate, or student of political science to know this. Just look at what went wrong in Zimbabwe under President Mugabe, Ghana under President Nkrumah, and Cuba under President Castro (to mention but a few), as well as what is going wrong in most of the Arab Spring and pre–Arab Spring countries under their various dictators or newly elected leaders that have arisen from their respective freedom movements.

But for some two decades now, no such thing has gone wrong with or happened to the ANC, which is a tremendous achievement not to be underestimated. And let us repeat that Nelson Mandela brought this about by reason of his famous and highly intelligent aforesaid culture of patient compromise, the liberal-humanist virtues and values of which he managed to convince most of his followers.

Even so, it cannot be denied that the one thing that he did fail to do was to achieve an urgently required new deal for the desperately needy and hungry underclass, for the improvement of which he has prepared the ground, certainly, but without, as yet, a new deal sealed on their behalf, even after some two decades of ANC government. Which is why it now remains for President Zuma to find a way of doing this—easier said than done!—if much or all of what Nelson Mandela stood for is not to be blown away.

While this underclass was released from apartheid, it was not, alas, released from its poverty trap (how could it be, in the absence of Communism or something similar, and even then?). Not that most apartheid and other South African whites have lost too much sleep over this underclass either—why would they?—as they have accepted it with a shrug and busily gotten on with their lives and their bank balances. But they have, predictably, used it as a political stick with which to beat the ANC and to perpetuate the usual racist propaganda against it. Whether the underclass is listening to them is doubtful, given that President Zuma is currently very popular with most blacks still, notwithstanding all the mud that has been thrown at him (apart from a few in the black middle-class elite that have gone over to the whites, as have some middle-class Indians).

Because the world has seen all these underclass problems before—in France prior to the French Revolution, in Russia and China prior to their Communist revolutions, and in India and Pakistan where next to nothing has been done for the respective underclasses—there is absolutely nothing new about these tired old problems. But what is new in South Africa currently is that the writing is now on the wall and staring everybody in the face! There have also been underclass problems in the United States and Britain, albeit for a far less desperate underclass these days, but a dreary, deprived, and potentially angry and violent underclass for all that.

So what else is new in this wearisome world and its long and weary history on the dark side of the moon? What was certainly new under Mandela was the trusting nature of the black South African underclass and the spell that he cast upon it. But with the spell gone now along with its caster and with patience running thin, it remains to be seen what will happen. Is South Africa sitting on a powder keg, or is it not? Archbishop Desmond Tutu certainly seems to think so, to judge from his dire warnings.

In which case, if the keg explodes, will the ANC then revert from being a very superior freedom movement that turned itself into a proper government and become an extreme and despotic dictatorship or government instead? This would be unlikely, but when powder kegs explode, all kinds of unexpected things happen.

Freedom movements want freedom because it is what they fight and suffer for. They want it not only for their members, but also in order to live up to their ideals, with which they hope to change the world and make it a better place. But ultimately, once they have gotten their freedom, the question is whether their members will let them have it as they want it, especially if they fail to live up to their promises, or if they will completely abandon their ideals. However much they are against a lack of freedom—if only on deeply held principle—will their members let them have it if the freedom that they preach isn't working anymore or is being abused or neglected? Or will their members suddenly start to dictate a new and less free set of terms?

One cannot have been in political journalism for a few hours—let alone a goodly number of years, as I have—or have read one's political history and not be aware of this. It is a glaringly open secret! Not that it usually suits the politically correct in a freedom party or movement to admit this. But, sooner or later, we have to be correct rather than politically correct, which is the problem for closed political minds that are too often politically correct without being correct.

But, having said all this, it would seem that there are enough of these passionate freedom people remaining in the ANC today who have the intelligence, wit, and the antennae—not to mention the background and education—to know this better than most and to prize the freedom that has been bequeathed to them. They understand that the freedom that they have can only be kept by living up to their ideals, one of which was (unless it was mere rhetoric) to solve the problems of their underclass. But not, apparently, to solve them with all possible speed, which could be the undoing of the ANC if it does not now pull its finger out in double-quick time, for fear of a rogue elephant coming along! It is not yet clear that a rogue elephant—such as a Mugabe, for example—could trample over everybody else in the ANC, bullying and terrifying them into submission, if he took it into his head to do so. This is not Zimbabwe that we are talking about, but Nelson Mandela's South Africa, the fine traditions of which have been cleaner and stronger from the word go (the only secret armies in South Africa today are, reportedly, the remaining white apartheid armies out in the bush).

While there is no shortage of detractors and critics trying to unseat President Zuma behind the scenes, it doesn't follow from this that either they or he wants to turn the ANC into the private fiefdom for a tin-pot despot. But it does follow that Zuma's political enemies, especially whites who are racially prejudiced against him, will use scare tactics to this effect in order to unseat him. But in whose favor? These are early days yet, so Mandela fans will have to resist the temptation to panic and bide their time shrewdly and intelligently in the very best traditions of Nelson's culture of patient compromise—but not too patient, and not compromising too many of his ideals with which to help the underclass before it is too late. What is required is a messiah!

Speaking of which, when Nelson Mandela first came to power back in 1994, he told a local newspaper that interviewed him that he was no messiah; and he no doubt said this for the very good reason that he knew from the adulation and expectation that was being heaped upon him by millions of hopeful blacks, that far too much would be expected of him, and the unreality of their expectations could not be easily or at all fulfilled. Clearly, Nelson Mandela was not unaware of the enormity and perhaps the impossibility of the hopeless under-class task ahead, or indeed of the extent to which his presumed or hoped-for powers could easily become mythical if he did not watch out. Which is why, true to his aforesaid "always tell the truth about yourself" motto, he truthfully told people that he was not the messiah that perhaps they thought or hoped that he was, or were expecting—not he, or anybody else for that matter, one might add. As much as his fans and admirers wanted him to be a messiah, he reminded them that he was a mere mortal for all that.

Even so, unreality and myth were heaped upon him by a great many of his fans and admirers, so in a way he was stuck with their unreal expectations of him. He could hardly tell them grow up, think again, or dream on. He was their hero and leader and they expected him to behave accordingly with the very obvious heroic qualities that he had in spades; and this is what he did, using all his discipline and inner resourcefulness in the heroic service of his people to whatever extent he could continue to realistically serve them in the very difficult task that confronted them in future. This was the new task and the new challenge, not of getting rid of apartheid anymore, but of making the country and also the underclass work. How could one make the latter less of an underclass?

Apartheid was over, and the rules of the game were very different from there on, and not least with regard to making the economy work and managing it well for all the extra demands that were being put on it by all the extra blacks—millions of them—who wanted a slice of the action and a long-awaited piece of the pie. Those who represented them in the ANC's freedom movement came in all shapes and sizes and with all kinds of different ideas about what should and could be done or what was even possible. It was like a gathering of the clans. There were exiled blacks from abroad, blacks released from jail in South Africa, blacks who had been underground, and others who had been aboveground. There were opportunists out for their main chance and a fast buck, as well as idealists, cynics, pragmatists, and selfless people. And then there was Nelson Mandela (thank God!).

There were Socialists, Communists, capitalists, Westernizers, and Africanizers. Rogue elephants and kindly elephants from inside and outside the country, loose cannons, wild cards, sharp shooters, and pea shooters, you name it. They were all there, and they all thought they knew best, or they would have thought they knew best had it not been for the fact that most of them seemed to agree that Nelson Mandela knew best. So leave it to him and see what transpires. He does seem to have a magic wand, doesn't he? He's just being modest when he says that he is not a messiah, isn't he? Of course he is a messiah! Just look at what he has achieved.

The ANC was a mixed marriage of the compatible and incompatible, like all movements and political parties, and it was a keen-eyed Nelson Mandela who steered his way through these opposites, always with a clear eye on the future and reconciling different factions—just as his father had done before him when Nelson was a young boy watching and hearing about his father counseling the different tribesmen and keeping an eye on what was going on in the court of the tribal king.

If his father has been looking down from those holy heavens above, in which most of South Africa's blacks believe, he will doubtless have been proudly astonished by Nelson's achievements. Now that his Christian son has gone to the heavens above, it remains to be seen whether he, too, will be looking down with pride on future ANC leaders or turning in his grave instead.

And here we are now—on the occasion of Nelson's death in 2013—thinking about his legacy and what he has managed to bequeath to his nation with his presumed magic wand. This book argues that what he bequeathed most of all was his tremendous moral superiority and amazing culture of patient compromise that he brought about, including the interracial unity that came with it. Not bad going for the genius of one man, if you ask me.

But a single unanswered question still remains about Mandela's legacy—how come more wasn't done for the underclass? Did Nelson Mandela collaborate too much with those Western and other capitalists who couldn't care less about the underclass? Under Thabo Mbeki, who succeeded Mandela, the yawning gap between rich and poor widened while the economy raced ahead, leaving the poor even more woefully behind than before. By all accounts, this was the chief reason for the downfall of Mbeki in 2008 when he was obliged to resign.

While doing everything for the economy—which, to his credit, he liberalized and grew by a healthy 4.5 percent per annum (much better than the current rate of growth)—and while also doing much for a new black and very elitist, rich middle class, he did absolutely nothing for the poor. When Mbeki fell from grace, Nelson Mandela was able to stand back and remind his party elders, if they needed reminding, that it was they who had chosen Mbeki as Nelson's deputy and eventual successor, not he.

They had brought Mbeki on their own heads, presumably because they regarded him as a scholar, with his BA degree in economics from Sussex University in England and his economics MA from the University of London. This reputation is how he became the "executive" face of South Africa and distinguished himself in executive matters, including a new trade pact with Brazil, Russia, India, and China, and arguing that there was such a thing as "global apartheid" that needed to be overcome, in a world in which the rich nations were set economically "apart" from the rest. But he did nothing concrete for the remaining "apartheid" of the desperate millions in his homeland, on his doorstep, and in his own backyard!

But to his credit, his trade pact with Brazil, Russia, India, and China resulted in 2013 in the setting up of a new international development bank in South Africa and with the inclusion of South Africa as a partner—called the BRICS bank, an acronym for Brazil, Russia, India, China, and South Africa—which should be good economic news indeed for South African economic development from here on.

While some fear the political influence and interference of Communist China and Russia in South Africa's political and financial affairs, there seems to be a good political balance within BRICS, with both India and Brazil in on the deals, not to mention South Africa itself. So no one nation should be able to wield more political or other influence than another, and the others are always free to oppose anything to which they object. And the fact is that now there will be, hopefully, substantial amounts of desperately needed Brazilian, Russian, Chinese, and Indian monies that are not coming into South Africa from any other source, as well as trade deals and manufacturing expertise (the latter especially from India and already underway)—all of which can and will help to generate more wealth and many more jobs for ordinary or poor blacks. And with the United States suddenly looking for an economic role in Africa, following President Obama's 2013 tour, there should be new US deals on the horizon before long.

That Mbeki was a scholarly intellectual, nobody seems to doubt, and there is general agreement that his economic management and planning was good, but it was his amazing and well-publicized blunders that brought him down, with regard to his alleged neglect of AIDS, the poor, and his power struggle with Zuma that got him nowhere fast. With a reputation for being an aloof man, Mbeki was no Mandela. But none of this takes away from his worthy economic achievements that are not to be underestimated, the consequences of which—including what to do about the underclass—were always going to take time, which unfortunately ran out for Mbeki.

The South African underclass was Nelson Mandela's *miserables*, with whom they are compared in this chapter—for the purpose of drawing an historical parallel with their earlier French counterparts—in order to highlight the real nature and panhistorical perspective and significance of their problem, indeed the world's eternal problem. There's always an underclass in the economic history of all countries. The rising tide of all rising economies, all over the world, does not, alas, float all boats—on the contrary, it sinks some of them and leaves others stranded on the shore.

This is true of the rising economies in Africa today that are not sufficiently inclusive to float the boats of their respective underclasses, and it has been true of South Africa since the ANC first came to power. As for the declining and sinking economies in Europe, Britain, and the West, well, even more boats are being sunk!

So this underclass problem is not just a South African problem, out of sight and out of mind, but a world problem, and all races and nations have been there, and not least France whose famously infamous underclass problem triggered a history-changing revolution in that country. This is what underclasses can do. They can trigger revolutions for good or ill if their inequalities and injustices are not dealt with, and we would do well not to forget this.

Western readers will be more familiar with European underclasses than with black underclasses, and they will be more familiar right now with a revolutionary French underclass because of the *Les Miserables* Oscar-winning film that was released and in the news in Britain, the United States, and Europe in 2012. Which is why right now is a good time to talk about *Les Miserables* and its relevance to the underclass problem in South Africa and the world at large today.

The French story of France's nineteenth-century underclass is based on the longest-ever stage musical in London's West End, so there are many in Britain and Europe who really should know how terrible it was to be one of the *miserables* in France and what the consequences can still be for such people and countries. When the celebrated French novelist Victor Hugo wrote the novel on which the stage musical and the film are based, he commented on the need for books such as his (just as there is still a need for such books today, especially about South Africa's *miserables*).

He argued that "for as long as there shall exist, by reason of law and custom" what he described as "a social condemnation . . . that artificially creates a hell on earth," which in turn "complicates with human fatality" [and one might add frailty!] as well as a terrible "destiny," then expect the worst! Expect it because the worst is being done to those who are socially condemned. This is a very timely message for a world in recession, as well as for the socially condemned millions in South Africa. Victor Hugo knew it back then, and we should take warning in the here and now.

And, as we know, the French certainly got the worst with their bloody revolution, but they also got eventually the best of it, which is more than can be said for other great and terrible revolutions of history with much bloodletting. Victor Hugo could have been talking just as well about South Africa in later times (not that South Africa and its blacks could have been further from his thoughts!), first under apartheid and currently under the ANC from which the black underclass deserves and urgently needs better.

I mention this in this chapter to seriously underline that what is happening to the desperately poor blacks in South Africa and Africa today is remarkably similar to and much worse than what happened to French peasants in nineteenth-century France, who started their revolution in which they showed no mercy to their oppressors (while South Africa's blacks have, thus far, shown mercy to their former apartheid oppressors), whose upper- and middle-class French heads fell thick and fast under the sharp cut of the French guillotine.

When Victor Hugo also spoke of the "degradation of man" by the "exploitation of his labor" and also of the "ruin of women by starvation," again he could just as easily have been talking about South African blacks today. There is no difference, except for the skin color, time period, and culture of the oppressed French in France and the oppressed blacks in South Africa. But the human problem, the moral problem, and revolutionary-outcome problem are just the same as that emphasized by Victor Hugo, and not least with regard to the "atrophy of childhood" and also to the "social asphyxia," so long as "ignorance and misery remain on earth." All this and more are applicable to Nelson Mandela, Thabo Mbeki, and President Zuma's *miserables* today, just as it was applicable to apartheid's *miserables* previously. This is a miserable community that is centuries old.

Because these historical parallels have a clear relevance and message today that underlines the just and worthy cause of the poor that it is dangerous indeed to ignore and neglect—as it was way back in the days of the French Revolution—it is by no means a waste of space writing and reading about it in this chapter.

So heed Victor Hugo's words, if you will not heed those of Desmond Tutu. They are invariably and inevitably true, as ever, yet we never seem to learn from them or from history. How many more words do we need from the great and the good? Because all men—big and small—make their own history most of the time, they need to be careful of the history they make, but they do not always make it as they please (as Karl Marx suggested in 1852), because the history that they make is very often compromised or derailed. They may make a revolution as they please, or not as they please if they do not prefer to make one at all, and in either event things may not—and often do not—turn out as it pleased them to expect. They may neglect an underclass and not be very pleased with having neglected it when that underclass throws a wrench in the works!

But Nelson Mandela is one who finally made his own history, albeit after a tremendous struggle against cruel odds that were not in the least pleasing, and not without a goodly number of agonizing setbacks and experiences along the way.

One doesn't need to be an academic or economic historian to understand this—just read the newspapers, watch television, and see how history is made because it really matters. See it for what it is and can become for the worst if we don't watch out.

But as much as history matters, the historians can never account for long-term historical change. They have no more of a clue about why things change or will change, as so many things usually do, than you or I do, unless the changes in question are blatantly obvious, which they seldom are. Historians could not tell us whether apartheid would or would not end, when Soviet Communism would end, why or when the Berlin Wall would come down, or whether and when the world economy would go into recession.

And there's no reason why they should be able to tell us—history is not about predicting the historical future, only about recording the past and drawing whatever conclusions and lessons from it that seem to be reasonable and sensible (not that the lessons always get learned!). This is the infuriating thing about history, and if, like Nelson Mandela, you decide to take it on single-handedly, be prepared for it to blow up in your face, or for not being able to make your history as you would wish. The best that historians can ever do is record and analyze history's changes when they happen, not predict too many of them with accuracy.

They are like weather forecasters in this respect. They just don't have enough certainty of prediction to go on and, as always, there's a lot of bad weather out there, along with the good—a lot of bad people out there, along with the good.

And here ends this chapter and the moral of this chapter on the subject of Nelson Mandela's *miserables*! We are talking real *misery* here, so let's not forget it, and let's not neglect it at our peril. However, the remaining chapters in this book are all about President Zuma, the current president of South Africa—now that we have finished with the history that

Nelson Mandela endured and made while also having considered his legacy and having praised the man greatly in the first four chapters. From here on our story changes to a Zuma story and also a South Africa story.

Now that Nelson Mandela is no longer with us, it's all about President Zuma and others in the years ahead, and how well they adhere to the Mandela legacy.

CHAPTER FIVE

To Kill a President

I N THIS CHAPTER we move on from the late President Mandela—as he would surely wish us to do—and look to the future of South Africa under the current president of South Africa, Jacob Zuma, starting with quite a nasty shock!

Not a shock of President Zuma's making, I hasten to add, but a nasty shock for all that. The shock in question is the attempted assassination of President Zuma and other prominent black leaders by a bunch of Afrikaner whites who would, had this assassination succeeded, almost certainly have triggered a race war; the repercussions of which would have been horrendous, swamping South Africa in rivers of blood, and undoing absolutely everything that Nelson Mandela had worked so hard to avoid previously (we are back to men making history as they please again!).

For sure, these wannabe assassins would have wrecked Mandela's legacy. There were four of them—white South African racist extremists—and they were foiled in their evil and crazy attempt to assassinate President Zuma and other ANC leaders to overthrow the ANC government and party in South Africa in December 2012. This was when they planned to mortar bomb and hand grenade the then-forthcoming annual conference of the ANC and execute its leaders! As a result, people were painfully reminded that all is very far from well in certain white sectors and white racist political organizations in Nelson Mandela's rainbow nation that the great man founded some two decades ago.

Most South Africans—black and white—were so absolutely stunned and speechless that a noisy silence let forth an agonizing howl of silence! Hardly anything has been publicly discussed or debated about this in South Africa since! It's as if people have lost their voices or this ugly event has been put off-limits.

The four wannabe assassins in question were of course white Afrikaners, and one says "of course" quite simply because it is the white Afrikaner community—with its largely Dutch and German racial origins, and its recent nationalist apartheid history with its severely puritanical Dutch Protestant religion—where there are, alas, plenty of racist and fascist extremists to be found still. They are still to be found because they feel aggrieved for what has become of them after either falling to the bottom end of the social ladder in today's South Africa, or otherwise being no longer at the top anymore where, as racists, they believe that they rightfully belong! They are not

Indians, mixed-race coloreds, or blacks who are aggrieved and disgruntled, but white Afrikaners with a king-sized chip on their shoulders and a deep-seated anger and racial resentment into which they will have been indoctrinated from birth. There are a few, apparently, Irish-Afrikaners among them, but their Afrikaner community and racial history is decidedly Dutch or German, as are the ominous underground and other racist movements to which they belong.

At the bottom end of the ladder, these are the seriously backward whites who have stubbornly refused to move on with the times and enter into the spirit of the rainbow nation. Most of them are from poor white communities—but not desperately poor like their black counterparts in the shantytowns—and not so very poor, because many volunteer as "soldiers of fortune" to go into other South African countries to help overthrow black governments there, or otherwise receive funds for their cause from wealthier South African whites or from white racist organizations in the West (the United States' Ku Klux Klan has been mentioned).

I have visited some of these backward people in their white backwaters, off the beaten track in their seriously down-market hillbilly districts (in outer Pretoria for example), and they are not a pretty sight. Drinking with them at the bar or in the grounds of their pubs is like drinking with Nazis in Hitler's Germany back in the 1930s.

There are rumors of greater numbers of them out of sight and mind, out in the remote villages and towns in the distant and hidden South African bush somewhere, with military arsenals of machine guns, rifles, pistols, explosives, and rockets, and their tin-pot white warlords with their tanks and other military vehicles, still preaching their race hate and desire for race war. They are the shameful past of the Dutch-Afrikaners—the skeletons both in and out of the closet—firmly opposed to a racially harmonious future. It was December 2012 at the forthcoming ANC annual conference in Bloemfontein where a handful of them tried to make some ugly history of their own—as it pleased them, but it did not work out as it pleased them. They had prepared to strike without realizing that President Zuma's police force, spies, and intelligence service were onto them and ready to pounce, which is why they are now being held behind bars.

How they were found out and apprehended remains a secret. People are guessing, of course, but the canny Zuma government is, as yet, not telling. Just as the Irish Republican Army (IRA) from Northern Ireland once upon a time targeted Prime Minister Margaret Thatcher and her government at the Tory party annual conference at the Grand Hotel in Brighton in October 1984—blowing up the hotel and tearing it apart with long-delay time bombs, only narrowly failing to kill Prime Minister Thatcher and her husband Dennis in their bedroom—so these hideous white Afrikaners planned to emulate them at a time when the ANC conference was about to celebrate the one hundredth birthday of the ANC. Had they succeeded, one can well imagine the awful difference it would have made to the sad news of Nelson Mandela's death.

These Afrikaner equivalents of the IRA (equivalents in their own estimation) are great admirers of the IRA, whom they romanticize and imitate, as are the Afrikaners who approve of them or secretly support them. There is a great ignorance about the English and the IRA in South Africa's white community where, at many levels—socially respectable, intelligent, and otherwise—they see the IRA as oppressed fellow whites at the hands of the English and British, just as they regard themselves as oppressed South African whites at the hands of the blacks these days, and the English and British before the blacks, once upon a bitterly remembered time.

And many of these South African whites do not even understand that there is a political, religious, and racial difference between the chiefly Scottish (by descent), Protestant Ulster-Irish in the North of Ireland and the Catholic Irish and IRA in or from the South. They ignorantly think, many of them, that North and South in Ireland are or recently were both the same, united against the English—of which they wholeheartedly approve—and that the Ulster-Irish in the North are bosom pals of the Catholics and the IRA in or from the South! But it suits them to think that they have an affinity with the Irish and the IRA of North against the English, and they will not believe for one moment that the Ulster-Irish in the North are Unionists who are flag-waving pro-British and pro-English Union Jack people, who want or have wanted nothing to do with the Irish in the South or the despised IRA.

These are not people who watch or follow much international news or read into history books. They are simpletons and backwoodsmen who believe what they want to believe from what they have heard; what they generally believe is that they are the natural running mates in this troubled world of the Irish and the IRA against the "nigger-loving" English who are their enemies, as well as the enemies of the Northern Irish (whom the English have been supporting and protecting for half a century and more, and whose loyalty they have received for the same amount of time!).

But, while the more experienced and skilled IRA in the United Kingdom succeeded in killing five British politicians at the Tory party conference in Brighton in 1984—but no government ministers—and also succeeded in injuring thirty-four others, including the prime minister's former secretary of state for employment and also the trade minister, Norman Tebbit, and his wife Margaret (both of whom were permanently disabled)—their less experienced white Afrikaner counterparts had no such luck in Bloemfontein, because they were swiftly rounded up, mercifully before they could do any harm. They had hoped to take President Zuma and as many other black ANC leaders as they could outside and publicly execute them!

The terrorism in South Africa is the kind that goes back, in spirit, to Boer War and Dutch settler days, as well as to the glory days of rigid and well-organized apartheid after the British left the country to itself in 1948 when, as we have seen, apartheid really came into its own, as did the Afrikaner National Party that turned South Africa into an unchallengeable one-party state. There are so many skeletons in Afrikaner and apartheid closets still, weird and fanciful ghosts with which to capture the lurid imagination of these white terrorist revolutionary lunatics who have tried to assassinate President Zuma and other ANC leaders. These are racist lunatics who are living in a different time and place, far removed from the twenty-first century, as they dream their impossible dreams of grabbing some self-determination with which to become segregated out of black Africa (they want their own independent state).

The ANC conference at which the accused wannabe assassins were hoping to pounce was, they believed, a sitting duck, as they went armed to the teeth—Mark Trollip, John Martin Keevy, Hendrik Prinsloo, and Hein Boonzaaier, reportedly—but only to get themselves immediately arrested en route and charged with high treason and a terrorist conspiracy in the Bloemfontein Magistrates Court. Had they succeeded in their mission, the Bloemfontein fountain of flowers (which is what "Bloemfontein" means) would have been flowing with a fountain of blood.

Forty-eight-year-old Mark Trollip is from Johannesburg, and forty-eight-year-old John Martin Keevy is from Port Elizabeth, South Africa's naval capital, while forty-nine-year-old Hendrik Prinsloo and fifty-one-year-old Hein Boonzaaier are from Centurion in Pretoria. They were arrested in Bloemfontein and various places en route to it, or from which they came, suggesting that President Zuma's police were on to them early. But had this ominous gang succeeded in assassinating ANC leaders, a very big wrench would maybe have been thrown in the works in the form of a revolution—chiefly along racial black and white tribal lines. And what a shocking disaster that would have been for South Africa, which is what these extremists wanted.

According to reports, three of these crazies are, predictably, members of extreme right-wing Afrikaner organizations. Prinsloo was the leader of the Blanke Boere Forum (BBF), which in turn is reportedly part of the Volks Vereniging Organisasies. The others are thought to be members of the Wit Brandwag and a recently formed Federal Freedom Party. They are supposed to have their own highly armed cowboy-terrorist units with great arsenals hidden away in remote but readily accessible regions. If they had succeeded in killing off the ANC leadership, they expected that the nation and the ANC would have been so stunned that their armed supporters would have come crawling out of the woodwork and responded to a nationwide call for a revolution. It seems that their plan was to create a bloodbath at a so-called "Battle of Mangaung" before the expiration of the ANC conference, with the aim of "murdering the black South African nation" and getting self-determination for the old "Boer nation."

Because the ANC leaders were scheduled to dine at the University of the Free State in Bloemfontein, it appears that this is where they were to meet their intended deaths or arrests if they survived the bombs and gunfire. The idea was to eliminate the leadership of South Africa and the ANC in one fell swoop! Cell phones, firearms, and laptops were all confiscated by the South African police that foiled these planned assassinations and, again reportedly, emails showed that the right-wing leader of the Gereformeerde Republikeine was in the picture, if not actively in the frame.

It would seem that President Zuma should execute these terrorists for their attempted murderous treason, or otherwise imprison them for life, but he and his government have suddenly gone quiet about this matter—as have virtually all sectors of the white press in South Africa that are not exactly falling over themselves to investigate or follow this unsavory story (almost as if they are too embarrassed to do so)—this story that has, incredibly, not made world headlines.

Can you imagine how the British press would relentlessly pursue such a matter in the United Kingdom?

No doubt the anti-Christian public statements that President Zuma made in 2012—reportedly claiming, among other things, that all Christianity ever did for South Africa was to give it missionaries and old people's homes (and, one could add, apartheid)—had enraged these wannabe assassins, not that this in any way explains or justifies the evil that they planned. Zuma has also been publicly critical of whites who spend more on their household pets and their vets than on their black gardeners and domestic staff. But whatever he has said to increase racial tensions between whites and blacks—that Nelson Mandela would not have said and did not say previously—it in no way accounts for or justifies those with their tiny racist minds whose aim it was to kill him and his ANC colleagues.

Because President Zuma is a Zulu and not a Christian, one cannot expect him to be a great cultural or religious fan of Christianity—otherwise he would have converted by now in his seriously religious nation—not that his apparent anti-Christian sentiments are falling on anything but deaf ears in black, overwhelmingly Christian South Africa today.

Just as there are good and bad Christians, there are good and bad Zulus likewise, so it's by no means clear that these anti-Christian sentiments have been welcomed even by the Zulu community (for whom, perhaps, they were intended) that still believes in Nelson Mandela's rainbow nation.

CHAPTER SIX

Good and Bad Zulus and Good and Bad Dutch-Afrikaners

Now I HAVE a story to tell about two extremes—good and bad Zulus and Dutch-Afrikaners, both of whom have been seen in fairly equal proportions since 1948, with the one (the bad white Dutch-Afrikaners) preceding and leading to the other (the bad black Zulus), and both occasionally overshadowing all the other good guys in between in their respective communities!

The story told here is by a good black Zulu taxi driver friend of mine living and working in South Africa, where he has converted to Christianity, and telling it as he sees it and knows it, in his own way. It sounds plausible enough to me to be included in this book because it gives one a very different and interesting perspective.

Most visitors to South Africa—and those living there—do not get to know their black taxi drivers very well, if at all, and do not keep in touch with them for several years, as I have kept in touch with this driver. So they don't know what their drivers are really like, what they know or think, or how they live. They simply have no idea about them. I have had nothing but good experiences with black taxi drivers in South Africa on all my visits during the past decade, and I am introducing one of them to readers now because it seems to me that he has some seriously interesting insights and experiences to offer that increase the racial and social dimension of our understanding of his country.

This extra dimension provides us with a better comprehension of the nature of the racial and other problems in South Africa today; what President Zuma—or any other South African president for that matter—is up against. It also provides us with a better idea of what the late Nelson Mandela and his successor President Thabo Mbeki had to keep in mind about the people they represented in the black and white communities respectively; both with regard to what they feel about each other across the racial divide and what the problems on the ground are for ordinary people.

The value of including this taxi driver in this way is that he is not at all untypical of so many other black South Africans at his employment and social level, black "others" who, just like him, deserve better and are trying to improve their lot—not just other taxi drivers like him, but other similar workers who decide which way to vote and what to make of their country and its recent racial history. They also decide whether to turn to crime or not in order to solve their financial and social problems that are not, as yet, being solved for them by ANC governments, just as they had no hope of their problems ever being solved for them by the white apartheid governments that went before.

It is ordinary people, such as this Zulu taxi driver, who are a pleasure to talk to and who are significant in the greater scheme of things. They are people who signify in terms of their civilized and caring behavior, their hardworking lives and economic conduct in the service of their nation, and the political and religious voices that they give to their communities and country. Naturally, this all depends on what life and their racial and social histories have done to them, and how they feel about it and interpret it.

They are the little people who can make a big difference to their politicians, with their own views of what is right and wrong with their fellow men—black and white—and what is likely to happen and why in their country. The inclusion of such a man with a true story to tell in these pages strikes me as being invaluable if we are to get to the heart of the matter with a racial *feel* for the lives of ordinary people on the ground.

While this Zulu taxi driver may or may not be a paragon of virtue in his private life, of which I know nothing, we shall see that he is clearly and essentially a good and decent man on whose shoulders (and the shoulders of millions more like him) rests the future of South Africa. Just like any London cabbie, he is a source of invaluable information, and he has his own opinions with which we may or may not agree, which is exactly why I have been pleased to feature him in this book.

Some four years ago, most of the taxi services and their black drivers in South Africa had not cleaned up their act, as many have today, so one had to be very discriminating indeed when booking a taxi, and certainly did not hail any old one that came along on the street, for fear of being abducted, hijacked, mugged, murdered, or raped. This still remains the case today to a certain extent. But there are many more safe choices on offer today from many more secure taxi services and their respectable drivers who really have cleaned up South Africa's taxi-driving act.

Interestingly, compared to the World Cup in Brazil in 2014, South Africa has proved to be safer and better managed for soccer fans from all over the world than has Brazil, thus far, where there has been rape and violent crime against visitors to Brazil in the run-up to the World Cup there, most shockingly involving the Brazilian police in league with criminals! There have also been violent political protests in Brazil, none of which happened in South Africa when it hosted the World Cup in 2010. So, full marks to South Africa and its black ANC government for that. They put on a safer, better, and more civilized show. Black South Africa in 2010 turned out to be much safer for soccer fans and visitors from abroad, and much better managed and policed, and the late Nelson Mandela turned out for the event to promote it globally as well as nationally.

But, to this day, the thing to remember in South Africa is never to take a taxi that has not been carefully vetted and is therefore not under contract to a known and respectable hotel, restaurant, or company that has your absolute safety (and future custom or business) in mind, and to whom you have recourse. One cannot be blasé about the choice of taxis. One has to pay attention and take care. But more than three to five years ago, one had to do a lot of looking and searching for such taxis, asking trusted people who could confidently recommend one. However, there are plenty on offer today, as long as you identify the right ones, most of which can be trusted as long as you follow the carefully prepared procedures for your safety (even so, let's not get carried away, but do tread with care!).

I have taken such taxis—luxury and air-conditioned and in complete safety—in such places as Durban, Johannesburg, and Cape Town—and each and every driver has been educated, friendly, very protective, and a pleasure to know, as they have driven carefully. But, as I say, it was not forever thus. And now there is one driver in particular whom I want to tell you about that I took in the bad old days when safe and air-conditioned taxis were few and far between.

Like President Zuma, he is a Zulu, but unlike Zuma, he has converted to Christianity, and he provides us with a "genre picture" about a taxi driver and his family in the down-market community in which he lives (we shall have other such pictures—in miniature or otherwise—before we are through with this book, providing us with real insights or glimpses into the lives of ordinary people in passing). I used this driver's vetted and recommended taxi service on several occasions, and I made copious notes after the different journeys that I took with him, with a view to writing a book some time later. I usually make notes of what it is that people have told me after I have parted company with them, regardless of whether or not I am writing a book or an article, especially when the stories they tell and the comments they make are too priceless to chuck away (it's an old journalistic habit). One never knows when these notes may come in handy later on when there are books or articles to be written. That's what writers do. They make notes, literally and also mentally, so don't be alarmed if you see them at it, apparently apropos of nothing!

My Zulu taxi driver drove his busy little taxi through the streets of the big city in which he lived with his wife and two daughters—I am not at liberty to name him, his family, or the city, given that he lives among violent people who might object to what he has told me about them—living and driving with an almost permanent smile on his face. It was a fixed smile, but not a fake one, just a natural smile that refused to die in the face of adversity; a smile that was bigger than his heart. He believed that he had reason to be smiling because he had escaped the horrendous squalor, lack of hygiene and sanitation, and crime-soaked poverty of South Africa's demoralizing and soulless shantytowns.

If you are black in South Africa and can find a way of avoiding the teeming degradations and severe hardships of the shantytown slums and their dwellers—living under leaky tin rooftops in makeshift lean-to hovels that are heaped with discarded bits of cardboard and linoleum, as well as bits of rejected or stolen carpet or mats filling in the gaping holes of the shacks and providing them with supports for their wobbly rooftops—if you can find a way of avoiding all this, I guess you have a big reason to have a big smile on your face! Such a rough and tumble—jumble and jungle—of human misery, decay, and depression can soon wipe the smile from your face.

Let us be clear. These are shanty homes with no drainage, clean water, or toilet facilities, and with dirt roads, so they are no laughing or smiling matter (even though you may find some people bravely smiling there).

In contrast to these places that are nothing to smile or write home about, my Zulu taxi driver had a gutsy grin and unfailing smile that came to him like a breath of fresh air. His was a smile that had smiled degradation, depression, despair, and horror right out of his life, heart, and soul, by taking to the road in his medium-sized taxi that was newly imported from India because it was less than half the price of other more luxurious cabs from Japan, Germany, and the Western world. And what's more, he had (and I hope still has) a great sense of humor to go with it. So he was also smiling because he really could see the funny side of things.

His car was a Tata—named after the famous Indian steel conglomerate that manufactured it—and it didn't have any air-conditioning. But he had cured this problem by driving with the windows open to let in the fresh air—together with the heat, dust, and exhaust fumes from other cars!—advising his passengers to wind up their windows while he left his open, so that they could breathe some hot or lukewarm air in the absence of cool air-conditioning!

He was nothing if not ingenious—he also had a second line of business repairing cell phones in his spare time. After he had taken to the streets in India's very robust and dependable "people's car" during the day that suited his pocket just fine (but not the comfort of his passengers!), he attended to his second line of business in the evenings. Instead of air-conditioning, his car had a silly little fan that stirs hot air in a feeble attempt to make it less warm (as I say, lukewarm), as he wondered what the Indian car manufacturer was thinking of (cutting economic corners was what it was thinking of, but no matter, Africa is Africa and India is India).

This taxi driver was typical of so many struggling against tremendous odds, trying to make his way in life. He apologized for his inadequate car, but explained that he could not afford a bigger and more luxurious vehicle with air-conditioning until he got more business. He also explained that he had worked in England and tried to bring a better car back with him from there, but that it was impounded by South African customs who slapped such a big import duty on it that he could not afford to pay it, so customs refused to release it. Perhaps he was hoping to modestly bribe someone in customs to release his car from England—given that he must have known of the import duty that he would have to pay. Perhaps they had unfairly added to the amount of the import duty; I have no idea. But, if so, the chances are that he could not afford a modest bribe either.

He was a lifelong fan of the Arsenal soccer team in North London that he supported from a distance, watching it on television in South Africa. He liked the club not least for all the brilliant black superstars that it brought from France or French Africa—Thierry Henry and so many others—which filled him with predictable pride, joy, and hope for blacks and black role models in the field of sports who could make some money in the West. Not that he had any plans to be a footballer himself, or expected to make too much money in his lifetime. He was in his mid-thirties and new to taxi driving, having worked as a gardener and also on building sites previously, but he had great hopes of going far in this cheap and affordable Indian taxi of his.

This is his story, as he told it to me, and as I understood it. If anything got misunderstood in the process of his telling it—or lost in translation between his African English and my white English—so be it, because it is a good story for all that, and an accurate one in most if not entirely all respects. We need stories such as his with which to develop a worldview that includes a view of South Africa lower down the social scale, and such stories, plausible, exaggerated, or otherwise, are better than no stories at all. We were not born yesterday, so we can make up our own minds about them.

Because his Indian car that was cheap has liberated our hero, as well as others like him, he figures that he has reason to be happy, but he has another reason also, and that is his belief, he told me, in his Christian God. Here he is, a God-fearing man of true moral fiber, a practicing Christian Zulu who sings in his church choir, he who has no business with black and violent Zulu criminals or crime, of whom there are far too many, of course.

Many black criminals are and very probably will remain his neighbors in the shabby and down-market, violent neighborhood in which he lives and sends his daughters to school. So, here he is, regardless of his lowly and dismal circumstances, a thoroughly decent and proud man who manages to look on the bright side of life and of his religion.

"When God is ready," he told me as I sat in the back of his taxi when we first met some four years ago—as he dodged in and out of the traffic jams ahead of us—"the heavens will open up in the sky above and angels will welcome us all. We shall all stop what we are doing and rise up with wings on our heels and fly off into the heavens. The dead will rise up out of the graveyards and fly to heaven along with the rest of us. It will be such a happy and merciful time that we shall all go and join the angels and love one another in one happy family. The dead will return to life from their graves in the ground to join this happy family in the Kingdom of Heaven in the heavens above. That is my vision and I often think about it and pray for it."

"Ah yes, fingers crossed," I replied.

"That is a very good English saying." He chuckled. "*Fingers crossed.* I like it very much, and let us hope so indeed. We must all cross our fingers and pray to God that His will shall be done. We must all love God and one another. And there is another English saying, which is *V for victory*, and we must all believe in victory if we are not to be defeated by the devil in this life. We must believe in the victorious nature of God to overcome the devil if we are to be saved. And we must also have a forgiving nature. Your World War II prime minister, Winston Churchill, always gave the V for Victory V sign, I believe."

I told him that this was quite right, but also of the other, very rude meaning of an English V-sign, so perhaps Churchill was giving that to Hitler also! My taxi driver roared with laughter after I explained this. I also told him of Winston Churchill's belief in the acronym KBO.

"What is the meaning of KBO?" he wanted to know.

"'Keep Buggering On!'"

This amused him greatly, and he roared with laughter yet again as he repeated the KBO letters to himself. His English was very good indeed—like that of so many English-educated Zulus and other blacks—and he was so fascinated by the language that he was keen to speak so well. He was a man of words and imagination with quite a rich vocabulary for one speaking in a second tongue. At home and in the Zulu neighborhood from which he came, he spoke Zulu, as we might expect, but other than that he spoke English, and he told me that he was teaching his daughters to speak English so that they could learn it better at school. The Afrikaans language he has refused to learn, for obvious historical and racial reasons. As we have heard already in this book, the Afrikaners in the days of apartheid tried to prevent the blacks from speaking English because they did not want them to have access to a global language with which to air their grievances and make their arguments and protests in the outside world in favor of human rights, democracy, and independence for South African blacks. The Afrikaners tried to force the blacks to speak their language instead of English, as a second language after their own tongue, but many of the blacks had none of it. He told me that it was the English-language world to which they wanted to belong, not the shameful Dutch-Afrikaner speaking world, so these blacks had been in no mood to be cheated or bullied out of speaking English by their racist overlords.

On one occasion when his taxi came to an abrupt halt in the traffic congestion and could move no further because there was a gridlock for miles ahead, he told me, "Forgiving, that is the big thing. We must all be more forgiving and understanding, that is what Nelson Mandela has told us. We must be good Christians and turn the other cheek."

"But there is so much to forgive in this world—too much."

"Yes, but we really must forgive each other here in South Africa for all the many racial and other sins, not only of apartheid, but of other things as well. That is what we blacks believe and have done, thanks to Nelson Mandela and Archbishop Tutu, who have preached God's word about forgiving and the need for us to turn the other cheek to our former white oppressors—another very good English saying and an excellent Christian thing to do, to *turn the other cheek*—otherwise we would have massacred all the white Afrikaners who enslaved us for so long before our independence, when they did so many bad things to us in the terrible days of apartheid. Really bad things. They called themselves white Christians! So how could they have done such un-Christian things to us?"

"The blacks have proved themselves the better Christians by far, that's for sure. The Dutch Protestant Church in particular has a lot to answer for. It swam in sewage and came out smeared with it."

"Yes, exactly! That's what it did. It swam in stinking sewage. These wicked white Afrikaner Christians will surely be punished by God. But it is not for us to punish them, it is for God, and it is for us to forgive, but it's not easy."

"But the blacks do well to do so, my friend. It is by far the wiser and more civilized course to take, the better moral, political, and economic option for all concerned, and let us hope that you will soon find a solution to your intolerable shantytown slums."

"The slums are still with us, as are most of the racist white Dutch-Afrikaners who have robbed us of so much and did so many bad things to us, condemning us to these slums by stealing all the wealth and the land—many of the older ones and also their children are still with us. Others have left the country for Britain or Australia, but others remain. Maybe their children are not to blame, but the parents and grandparents are. They are responsible in the eyes of God. We have not forgotten those days, or what was done to us by those people, but with God's help we have somehow managed to forgive and be merciful. Don't ask me how! It is very hard to forgive such things and such evil white people when our wounds are still in the tender and painful, very slow process of healing. I am talking about the Dutch Afrikaners, not the British; the British did us no great harm by comparison, after they had colonized us. They were the lesser of two evils and they did us a lot of good in the process of colonizing us, with their justice, education, Christian religion, free speech, and with sympathy for our plight and their moral support for us during the apartheid years. So many British people supported and helped us and were kind to us in the ANC's struggle for liberation, treating us like human beings. But not the racist Dutch-Afrikaners. They were very cruel and treated us like animals."

"But, hopefully, time is a great healer."

"*Time is a great healer.* Yet another of your wonderful English sayings! I do love your language. But they hurt us a lot, our former apartheid masters, so it will take a lot of time, and it has been almost impossible to forgive them. Yet we have generally managed to do so. We have managed—and are still managing—to heal the wounds. It is a miracle that we have found a way of forgiving them."

"Much to the Afrikaners' surprise and relief, no doubt."

There was a momentary silence as his magnificent smile slowly dissolved and disappeared from his otherwise cheerful face. "We have been forgiving these Dutch-Afrikaners since independence, with our truth and reconciliation programs, but still we do not like them or trust them for what they did to us. But if we are to be good Christians, then we must forgive for the sake of God and this newborn country of ours, which has nothing to gain from a bloodbath, because that would be hell on earth. We must not stoop to the un-Christian level of these un-Christian Dutch-Afrikaners. That is what we have been taught and what most of us believe."

Unlike many Zulus—but like the vast majority of other blacks—this taxi driver had converted to Christianity and put his tribal past and culture behind him. He certainly comes across as a sincere and passionate Christian with right on his side and some good points to make about the Dutch-Afrikaners. However, I decided to change the subject (with another genre picture). "You know what? I have a story to bring a smile back to your face. Listen to this. I saw some black Africans driving in a car here the other day in which there was a sticker in the back window that read 'Jesus loves us, we shall be saved,' and when their car stopped at traffic lights, another car behind it—whose black driver was driving too close and too fast—crashed right into the back of it, which suddenly made it look as though nobody was going to be saved!"

The smile swiftly returned to his face as he roared with laughter again. "Was anybody hurt?"

"No one."

"There you are, then, Jesus loved them and saved them."

"They certainly were saved."

"But the trouble with a great many of our black drivers in South Africa today is that they have no discipline and cannot judge distances. They drive too fast without looking where they are going and they don't keep in lanes because they are too impatient and very unruly. They just swerve around all over the place and bang into each other. You never know what to expect of them. We taxi drivers are better because our passengers are mostly Western and we don't want to lose their custom—cannot afford to lose their custom. Also the taxi drivers are better trained."

"The working- and lower-class blacks have no tradition of driving here," I suggested. "They are like Arabs and so many others in the third world where the driving is dangerous and bad because there has been no tradition of driving in those countries either. It takes time for these traditions with their disciplines, rules of the road, and attitudes of mind to be passed on from one generation to the next."

"Yes, that is it, no traditions or good attitudes of mind."

"Most British and European drivers usually keep in lanes and observe the rules of the road because they have been brought up to observe so many other rules and to toe the line in so many other aspects of their lives."

"What does *to toe the line* mean?"

"It is a phrase that means to conform to standards and rules, to keep in place and in line. To start at a starting line and end at a finishing line. To toe the line is what we call a figure of speech, which expresses things imaginatively rather than literally."

"Imaginatively rather than literally? So nothing to do with a person's toes then? But why imagine toes on lines rather than saying what you actually mean?"

"Well, it does have a lot to do with people's toes, as it happens, and it is often better to describe things to people imaginatively rather than literally because they remember them a lot better if the phrase captures their imaginations. The origin of *toe the line* in Britain comes from the seventeenth and eighteenth centuries—more than three hundred years ago—when British ordinary sailors in bare feet in the Royal Navy lined up daily for inspection by their superior officers with their toes all touching a line on deck where they were ordered to assemble, so that they could all keep in line perfectly and in good order in this way, instead of being out of line and all over the place."

"Why did they not have any shoes or socks?"

"Because they were too poor—only the officers had shoes and socks."

"Really? Too poor! British ordinary sailors?"

"That's right. White people in the West have known poverty way back in their history and many of them have been treated as inferiors by their so-called social superiors who have kept all the shoes and socks to themselves, which is why, when Westerners come here to South Africa, they should know better than to instinctively treat blacks as inferiors. But most of them either do not know their own history or, if they do, they choose to ignore it these days."

"But where did Royal Navy get the straight lines from?"

"They used existing straight lines between the wooden planks that had been laid and firmly fixed as flooring on the decks of their ships. So when they stood with their toes touching one of these plank lines, they all stood in a straight rather than a crooked line."

"How interesting! *To toe the line.* I really like this phrase and you are right; it is very memorable once you know what it means."

"Later on in history, soldiers on military parade grounds toed the line in their army boots when they all stood shoulder to shoulder in straight lines, just as athletes on racing tracks had straight lanes marked out on their tracks, lines that they had to keep to at avoid collisions, as well as starting lines to keep them all equal and in line at the start of a race. And there were more lines when they reached the finishing line. Horse racing tracks also had starting and finishing lines, of course, just as modern motorways have lines for drivers to avoid colliding with each other. So this is how the English language and culture has influenced everyday life, so very much for the better by getting good and useful ideas into their heads. This is how English phrases and ideas have traveled from one generation to the next, influencing their orderly everyday behavior and their understanding of how best to behave. This is the power and practical value of language and culture, and why people generally agree to toe the line in a good cause."

"Absolutely fascinating! I am going to tell my children about this. My Zulu neighbors need to toe the line much more than they do. But I doubt that they ever will, great fools that they are!"

"British children have toed the line in their school playgrounds where they have lined up for their teachers; the idea all goes back to those seventeenth- and eighteenth-century British sailors in their bare feet toeing the line for the first time in our history, as far as we know. Not many people know this, but we have twenty-five thousand idiomatic phrases of this kind in the English language—such as *keeping my head above water*, I've been *taken to the cleaners*, stop *pulling my leg*, and so on. But the thing about toeing the line is you've got to make sure that it is being toed for a good rather than a bad reason."

"Fantastic! I really like this language. But you mentioned idiomatic. What does that mean?"

"An idiom is a word that characterizes and typifies the nature of a certain culture and language and its people and is the special property of that culture and language."

"So it means the *special property* of a certain kind of language?"

"Exactly."

"We Zulus need much more of this kind of language and culture. I really love it. But most of my black Zulu neighbors in the rundown part of this city, where it is my accursed misfortune to live, are not educated and they are no good because they never toe any kind of line whatsoever in the interests of their race or our local community—unless they are bad lines. Some don't even bother to call themselves Christians. Others do, but still they still do bad things. They don't believe in the Ten Commandments, which they say are commandments for white men, not for them. These neighbors and their children are a bad influence on my children who have no choice but to go to school with them, and the school is no good because there is no discipline and the children do not learn."

"I'm sorry to hear this. What bad things do your black neighbors do?"

"They rob and kill each other, rape women, take drugs, and get drunk in the shebeens [pubs]. They have no self-respect, so they do not understand how to respect others. The men are brutal and out of control because they have guns and knives, so they just instantly shoot or knife anybody who upsets them, which is why most are scared of them and dare not to try to control or criticize them. Sometimes they put rubber tires around the necks of their black enemies or those they do not like in the streets where they live, pour gasoline over the tires, and set light to them, laughing as they burn people to death, watching their heads and faces go up in flames! They are very bad men."

"Not good news. So this country has gone from bad and stupid white men, to bad and stupid black men in this regard."

"Yes, it has gone from too many bad Dutch-Afrikaners to too many bad Zulus today. The good people, as usual, are in the minority."

"And what a very important minority they are, if the bad people are not to take over again, as they did before in the days of apartheid. . . . But do you know that things are going the same way in Britain among some whites in certain neighborhoods—albeit for far fewer numbers of people, but for similar reasons of moral and social decay. Not just in black neighborhoods, but in white neighborhoods as well."

"*Moral and social decay* is such a good way of putting it! I like that—moral and social decay. But this is not good news about your country. It is extremely bad news. . . . In this country our bad Zulu men are also out of control because our black police cannot be bothered with them or, if they can, they are corrupt and accept bribes from murderers, gangsters, rapists, and other criminals. Which is why aggrieved people occasionally take the law into their own hands and burn other people alive! By putting rubber tires round their necks—like a necklace—and then soaking them in gasoline and setting fire to them. But this is not the way to do justice. Can you believe that? Can you imagine it? I think that guns and knives should be banned in this country, but even then I expect there would still be killing, because a lot of people who don't have guns and knives just take bricks and smash their victims' heads in."

"One sees road blocks on the motorways where your black policemen are searching people's cars for guns and knives."

"Yes, and also for drugs."

"So much terror and grief."

"*Terror and grief* is right, terror and grief. Also, many people are dying of AIDS, which is grief of a different kind, and you will have heard all about this because it is well known. Some of the Zulu men here are so stupid that they even believe that they can cure this disease by raping little virgin girls."

"Have you or your wife and daughters ever been attacked?"

"Not yet. I try to avoid trouble and keep away from it, but it's not easy. When fellow Zulu minibus drivers cut me off on the open road, cursing and insulting me, I just ignore them and carry on minding my own business. If I cursed them back again, they would probably produce a gun and shoot me."

"Are you scared by what is happening?"

"Not for me personally—I am a Zulu, after all, and I don't scare easily—but my wife and two daughters, I fear for them."

My taxi driver was not a big man, as so many Zulus are. He was quite short, but he was powerfully built and strong enough.

"How old are your daughters?"

"One is three and the other five."

The gridlock suddenly broke and the traffic began to move again. The relatively short journey for which I had hired him was proving to be a long one on account of the heavy congestion. But at least there had been a very enlightening conversation in order to pass the time, thanks to this Zulu's English being so fluent.

He told me that he had been to a Christian missionary school—just like Nelson Mandela—where he was taught the English language so well that he now spoke it better than most Zulus at his low level of society who had not been to Christian missionary schools. With his cheap and cheerful car—and his cheap and cheerful smile to go with it—he had managed to distance himself from the dark and dismal shanty lands, festering in the bright sweltering sun, having provided for his wife and two little girls in the rundown back streets of the big city. The threadbare circumstances of the life in which I found him were marginally but simultaneously hugely better than the grinding slumland shanty poverty that still separates South Africa's poor from its not so poor. Where it still separates the teeming millions from the rest to whom a marginal difference is a huge difference.

Margins make a big difference in the lowly circumstances in which most of South Africa's blacks find themselves, in which a little goes a long way—a little extra money, a little kindness, a little sympathy and understanding from white visitors and expatriates, most of whom have no idea about the situation of lowly blacks in their different social sectors. They are distantly aware of them—because they see them from afar, or on the other side of the highway as they pass by, speeding in their cars—but they know very little about the appalling and intimate details. They can imagine what their lives must be like, but they cannot feel their pain and despair unless they have the necessary empathy, which many, alas, do not. They are left cold by it all, so they put it out of sight and mind.

"Your English is really good," I told him.

"Is it? Is it really good?"

"Yes it is. Very good indeed."

"I went to a good school, but did not matriculate, because my parents split up and could no longer afford to provide for me, so I had to leave school early and get a job as a welder."

"A welder?"

"Yes, on building sites. If my parents had stayed together, they could have kept me in school, but when they went their own separate ways, they needed money for other things. Especially my father, who was the main income earner."

"What did your father do?"

"He was an ordinary soldier in the white apartheid army of the Dutch-Afrikaners."

"How ironic."

"*Ironic?* What does that mean?"

"When we say or do one thing for an intended purpose, but it suddenly backfires on us and the opposite, unforeseen and unintended purpose results. Such as your black father joining the army of the Dutch-Afrikaners, presumably for the intended purpose of earning a living and making the country safe, but not for the unintended purpose of supporting apartheid later on and harming his own black people and oppressing them. That is what an irony is. Life is full of ironies of all sorts."

"I see. How interesting this word is—*ironic, irony, ironies.* I like this word very much. It is not only amusing but serious as well, because it makes us think about how things can go *seriously wrong* when they backfire on us and we finish up with the opposite of what we intended."

"That's right; this is the story of life so much of the time. But the word does not only apply to things that go *seriously wrong* when they backfire and one gets an unintended result, they can go *not so seriously wrong* as well, mildly wrong, but they still backfire, and that is when they are still ironic, but mildly ironic."

"Thank you for explaining this. I shall remember it. But there was no other army for my father to join, so he had to join the enemy in order to survive, and that is, as you say, very ironic! He would have preferred to join the British army if there had been one here for him to join. I never knew that I had an *ironic father* before! But he hated the white Dutch-Afrikaner army, so he left at the first opportunity."

"But why did he need to be a soldier?"

"It was the only thing he knew because he was a Zulu from a well-known tribe."

"Was your mother a Zulu also?"

"Yes."

"Does the tribe still exist?"

"Oh yes, very much so. There are a great many from my tribe at all social levels here in South Africa, including the highest. We are a very well-known tribe."

"Do you ever visit the tribe?"

"Not anymore. I have broken all my ties. I am the one who got away, no longer a Zulu. I have finished with the Zulus, as they have finished with me."

"Do you ever miss tribal life?"

"Not at all. I don't like all that ancestor worship, witchcraft, and cattle herding, and I do not like the fact that the Zulus did not support Nelson Mandela and the ANC, as did Nelson's fellow Xhosa and other tribes. Nor do I think that a republic like South Africa needs to have the status of the Zulu kings automatically enshrined in its constitution. The Zulus are an important tribe, of course, but not that important. They are Bantus like everybody else, yet they see themselves as superior, or something special, which makes no sense at all in this day and age. Most of them are impoverished migrant laborers in the big cities—laborers who have migrated to the cities in search of work and some food in their bellies. Others are well educated, like me. But the uneducated ones are always throwing their weight about and doing stupid things of which they are proud. *Throwing their weight about* is another of your English phrases that I like."

"You think they are too big for their boots?"

"Yet another of your English sayings that I like so very much! *Too big for their boots*! How many more of these sayings do you have? I should like to make a list of them. Yes, that is an excellent way of putting it, *too damn big for their boots*!"

"Are the Zulus still polygamous?"

"Polygamous? What does that mean?"

"Taking many wives."

"I see. Herding women like the cattle they used to herd. Not any more, not the migrant Zulus in the big cities, because they cannot afford it. Some in the tribal areas probably still are, among those that can just about afford it, but I don't really know, because I do not go back there. In their long history, the Zulus could not take a single wife until they had proved themselves in battle and attained a certain grade—a military pass mark. So the women hoped that their men would make the grade militarily so that they could then marry Zulu women who could get their husbands instead of staying single."

"So, if the men were wimps, no wife or wives for them!"

"What is a wimp?"

"A feeble and possibly cowardly or unmanly person."

"Ah yes, I see, that is a *wimp*. Very good. That is correct, no wives for wimps, ha, ha!"

As we see, my taxi driver was constantly marveling at the "wonders" of the English language to yield so many words, sayings, and phrases that he really enjoyed, this man who delighted in language for the sake of language and in conversation for the sake of conversation, whose sense of wonder at learning something new was like that of a child in a sweet shop.

I asked him, "So the Zulus had to demonstrate that they could use the military tools of their trade before they could think of using their other, smaller, and more intimate tools?"

"What intimate tools?"

"Between their legs!"

"Ha, ha! Yes, exactly! If they failed to use their military weapons, they were not allowed to use their sexual weapons either. I like your sense of humor, Englishman."

"My name is Bob, my friend."

"Thank you Mr. Bob. I would like to call you by your first name, it is so much friendlier."

He then asked me to call him by his first name, but I am keeping it to myself in the telling of his story in order not to reveal his identity to any in South Africa who may not appreciate what he has had to say about Zulus and Dutch-Afrikaners.

"The thing is about the Zulus," he continued, "life was very primitive and hard, and people could not help being brave and tough if they were to survive—and they were also superstitious—but they could only distinguish themselves as warriors, on the field of battle, which was not much of a life, especially after the British defeated them once and for all, when they had no choice but to go back to herding their cattle. But they had their famous pride, which remains to this day, and at least there were opportunities for the privileged few in the tribe— the chief's family, relatives, and hangers-on—to get a good education for their children. And I was educationally privileged, and always worked hard in school to make the most of my education."

"But I imagine that even hard work at school did not necessarily guarantee a successful life afterwards?"

"Quite right. Of course not, but some Zulus have done very much better than others who are no less educated than they are—people like me—and they have done better for all sorts of reasons other than their intelligence or education. They have even gone into government, law, and the civil service."

"It's the same in all races; some do better than others for all sorts of different reasons, and not just because they are better educated or more capable, much of the time, but because they have friends in all the right places to open doors for them, or to promote them above their station, or are just lucky."

"I have not managed to do very well for myself because I did not go into higher education, and this was as a result of my parents splitting up."

"But you are still fighting the good fight, living a decent life, and not accepting the violent and criminal or ignorant ways of so many of your neighbors."

"That's right. I never would accept such ways because they insult my intelligence and my dignity, which is important to me, even though their intelligence and dignity is not so important to them. Intelligence and dignity are gifts from God and we should not insult this gift or neglect it in any way. Thankfully there were many tribal chiefs and well-connected others in tribal days with a great many offspring who have managed to get a good or reasonably good English education and put their tribal past behind them. I count myself as one of the lucky ones in this respect. . . . But I am no longer interested in traditional Zulu customs and ways, which I regard as nonsense. For this reason I am not sure if I like President Zuma's closeness to the Zulus. I am a Nelson Mandela man, not a Zuma man. But we must wait and see how President Zuma turns out."

"You are a modern man."

"Yes. Some Western people have traditionally romanticized the 'noble savage' in their books and films about the Zulus, but I can tell you that there is not much nobility or dignity about Zulu or any other savages. It is a contradiction to believe so. There has been too much fighting, killing, and running wild, spilling blood, taking too many wives, and raping women. Yes, the Zulus were militarily and tactically very efficient on the field of battle. But where did it get them? They were only cattle herders after all. They did not wisely cultivate so much land, like Nelson Mandela's Xhosa people. I want better for myself and my family. I want a more civilized and sophisticated life. Oh yes, the Zulus are fearless and brave, but most are also stupid and they fight and kill too much for my liking and commit too many crimes. They are unruly."

"As I said, we have our own white Zulus in Britain. People who like fighting for the sake of fighting and who use violence to verify themselves and their manhood."

"*White Zulus*? Ha, ha! Very good. What does verify mean?"

"It means to check the figures to make sure they are correct, to confirm the truth of something, or to prove yourself in some way. Violent and manly people, with nothing else to offer other than their violence and their manhood, are bound to use their violence and manhood to verify themselves and establish the truth of who and what they are—brave and violent, stupid people. There are also cowardly violent people, but that's another story."

"Ah yes, I see—to *verify*. That is also what Zulus do. Too many of them love fighting and killing each other, or anybody else that comes along, to verify their manhood. Now, you tell me, how clever or honorable is that? So many of the gangsters and violent criminals in the big cities and the remote shanty lands today are Zulus. If you upset them, or argue with them, they will just pull a gun or a knife and kill you on the spot for the slightest difference of opinion. That's no way to live. I don't want to be a Zulu or be part of that anymore."

"Are the Zulus also the ringleaders and mafia bosses in the criminal world?"

"Not quite. They are up there with the best, but most of the ringleaders and bosses are Nigerians here in South Africa, who have come for a better life. They are into drugs especially, and they run much of the crime. But they cannot afford to upset the Zulus for fear of being wiped out by them, and they cannot control the many random crimes committed by Zulus who are up to their dirty necks in violent crime."

"What sort of crimes?"

"Zulu mafias run the taxis and minibuses that transport blacks to and fro and they wage turf wars with each other over territories. They do not run my taxi because I am a lone operator. But they would like to get their hands on it and my business, which is when I really do tell them to *go to hell*, as you English say! They also run protection rackets that people are forced to join and they hijack at gunpoint multistory residential blocks of rented apartments from landlords, forcing the residents to pay rents to them instead of the landlords, and then taking their commission before passing on what is left of the rent to the landlords! If they bother to pass on any of the money at all! We have so many recorded murders daily in this country—more than any other in the world, very probably— and goodness knows how many more that are not recorded, mostly black on black murders, and largely by Zulus. When whites are occasionally murdered by blacks, their deaths make the headlines in the press, but not when blacks are killed daily by other blacks."

"Dear, oh, dear."

"I know, that's Zulus for you. The landlords lose most if not all of their rents until such time as they go out and hire white South African heavies and their mixed-race security men to go and get the rented buildings back again and keep them out of gangster hands in future. These Zulus are as *bold as brass*, as you English say. They just march in and strut their stuff, hijacking entire blocks of apartments, putting guns to residents' heads and making them hand over their rents to them instead of their landlords. Can you imagine the horror? How bold and wicked is that? Zulus also break into the houses of the wealthy, robbing and stealing their cars, computers, television sets, passports, watches, jewelry, clothes—anything they can lay their hands on. Sometimes they kill their victims needlessly; other times they spare them as long as they are not opposed by them. They hide in the long grass at traffic lights and wait for a luxury car to stop there so that they can come out from hiding and put a gun to the driver's head in order to deprive him of his car and leave him stranded. That's why so many cars do not stop at red lights unless they positively have to. These criminal Zulus are a law unto themselves. That's why so many white neighborhoods are ring-fenced with so many security systems and heavily armed security guards."

"Yes, I have heard about their hiding in the long grass at traffic lights. Are there many white Afrikaner heavies engaged in the retrieval of the buildings that are hijacked from landlords?"

"There are some who are very heavy and nasty indeed. They also recruit rough and ready blacks and mixed-race people to assist them, paying them rather better than the black Zulu criminals pay their men."

"So the Zulus really are a force to be reckoned with in South Africa's ganglands."

"Most of them are nasty and very bad people, which is why I don't have time for them. They have lost their dignity and pride—how can they be proud of the way they live these days?—and they have become arrogant and stupid people, getting into arguments and killing others for the sheer hell of it. They are very bad Zulus."

"But you are a good Zulu."

"Ha, ha! Yes. *A good Zulu*, and you are a good Englishman, I can see that. Most of my passengers do not take such a lively or kindly interest in me or my race. You have sincere honest eyes. You are a good man. I have enjoyed our conversation. But we have reached our destination now."

I did, in due course, take a very kindly and friendly interest in my Zulu taxi driver when I used him on future occasions— buying surprise gifts, such as children's picture and short-story books for his two daughters, so that they could learn how to read and improve their English, and also a red and white Arsenal soccer club scarf and woolly hat for him to wear (this moved him almost to tears).

When he responded to an SOS from me to drive to a posh hotel out in the countryside where I had a white Afrikaner wedding to attend—but had forgotten to pack my best black shoes—he picked these shoes up from another hotel where I had left them behind and then raced them to me at the other hotel where the wedding was in process—and in the nick of time for me to attend the wedding. If he had arrived five minutes later I would have missed the wedding service unless

I had gone into church in my socks! On this occasion I absolutely insisted on ordering an excellent meal for him in the hotel (which the snobby black management did not want to serve to him, until I put my foot down!).

As his taxi drew to a halt after my first journey with him—and I had enjoyed the foregoing, very informative conversation, with him—I shook him warmly by the hand before getting out of his cab, while taking care to give him a good tip when I paid him.

"I'm very pleased to have met you and will certainly use you again," I told him. "We must keep in touch."

"I hope you will have need of me again before you leave."

"I will certainly use you before I leave, if you are free."

"For you, I shall always be free. Call me any time. You have my mobile."

And with these words and with yet another of his big moon-faced smiles, he took leave of me and went on his way as I waved him goodbye.

Not being a slum dweller or shantytown dweller—but a near-slum and near-shantytown dweller, rather—he was full of hope and courage for a better life to come, if not in this lifetime, then certainly in the next. For this hope he sings his heart out in his church choir on Sundays, when he is not giving his heart to his family or his care and attention to his passengers in this economically liberating Indian taxi of his that has enabled him to become a poorly paid king of the road and the streets (depending on how much money he can clock up). *King of the road*—he would like that! He does not wear his heart on his sleeve, by any means, but he is all heart when people talk to him and get to know him.

And that's the point; we can usefully get to know people—
can we not?—if we put ourselves out to talk to them and find
out about them and their lives and put ourselves in their shoes.
We can be genuinely interested in them and be prepared for
whatever they may tell us (why else am I a journalist, and why
else are you reading this?).

It is said that South Africa is a country in which a staggering 60 percent of young black males under thirty-five
years of age have never worked because there are no jobs for
them, which is doubtless why, it seems to me, so many turn to
violent crime instead. Unless they have a higher consciousness,
like the good Zulu taxi driver featured in this chapter, they
cannot rise above the dark and dismal spectacles and slummy
low-life visions all around them. But where will the higher
consciousness come from without a taxi or some other financially rewarding purpose in life to financially liberate them
and promote that higher consciousness at this low social level?

Without doubt, the Christian religion plays a seriously
important part in keeping a lot of blacks—Zulus and otherwise—on the straight and narrow in South Africa today,
keeping them decent, moral, and caring rather than violent,
criminal, and immoral. Of course, the same has been true of
whites in their history, but not of necessity anymore, because
there are these days so many other alternative routes to morality
and humanitarianism for whites, especially in Britain and the
rest of the white world. But for South African blacks, the
widespread necessity of the ever-popular Christian Church
among blacks seems to be absolute. With Christianity on their
side, the whites have the vast majority of the blacks on their
side, as does the Western world beyond the shores of South
Africa—there are few Muslims and pesky others to come and

hunt South African blacks and whites down or explode their bombs in public places or Christian churches.

It is estimated that 80 percent of South Africa's blacks are regular churchgoing Christians in a country in which an estimated six million civilians own firearms, many of which are unlicensed, which means that something like one in ten people owns a gun in a country in which domestic violence against women is widespread, and there is more male gun crime against women than men! This is a gun-culture problem that is worse than that of the United States, as well as a domestic violence problem.

Since meeting my black Zulu taxi driver some four years ago, I have kept in touch with him annually, and I have also met literally dozens of other blacks—including many other black taxi drivers—who sing the same tune as he about bad Dutch-Afrikaners and bad Zulus, if they are educated or converts to Christianity (which really does seem to be a *must* in black communities that have turned to the good), so I do not doubt—do you?—what they and my driver have been telling me. If what they are saying is not wholly true, it would seem that it must be largely true and that most of their impressions are valid, give or take one or two details here and there, and given that there is no smoke without a fire. By contrast, there is the legacy of the former badness of the Dutch-Afrikaners of the old white apartheid era in South Africa in the recent past running parallel with the latest badness of the black and largely Zulu and Nigerian communities in criminal quarters, the big difference being that the black atrociousness is not institutionalized racism, as was the former white. No doubt other black sectors are also criminally and violently involved, but the Zulus and Nigerians seem to be predominant. And then there is the reforming nature to the good of Christian rather than any or most other religions for the vast majority of the black population.

The question of whether South Africa's blacks have really forgiven the whites whom they were commanded by the late Nelson Mandela to forgive—whom they have apparently been forgiving for some two decades now—remains to be seen now that Nelson Mandela is no more. But there is another question of forgiveness also, as we shall see in the following chapter.

CHAPTER SEVEN

Have the Dutch-Afrikaners Really Forgiven the Dutch in Holland?

I N President Zuma's South Africa today, it is nothing less than incredible for people outside South Africa to get their heads around the fact that many of today's Dutch–Afrikaner whites still do not blame themselves, their parents, grandparents, or race for the apartheid and what was done to the blacks before the ANC came to power. On this issue, their Dutch courage has given them a thick skin and state of mind that makes no sense at all. It is presumably just as difficult for President Zuma and the ANC to fully understand this.

In my experience, far from feeling guilty, a goodly number of these whites—not all, but a significant number—still kind of blame the blacks for being black, when they are not blaming their Dutch cousins in Holland for disowning and washing their hands of them during the apartheid years; or they otherwise blame President Zuma for being the kind of black president that he is with the black culture and policies that he has. Many—not all, but many—are in complete and utter denial, and are also racially complacent, if not self-righteously and mildly arrogant with it, especially those who have been leaving the country to go and live abroad (generally speaking to live anywhere but Holland, from which their ancestors hail but where they are generally not overly welcome). Their racial and psychological condition is, to say the least, peculiar—peculiarly hypocritical and peculiarly Afrikaner-Dutch. How else to account for it?

Of course, they cannot afford to be more than mildly arrogant these days—apartheid has long gone, after all, so they cannot throw their weight about as before, and it is true to say that they are usually a very laid-back bunch of scoundrels—but their racial arrogance (and ignorance) is nonetheless readily detectable for all that. It is as starchy and simplistic as a lily-white Dutch bonnet or apron and as uncomfortable as a pair of wooden clogs (I have an Iranian friend in Amsterdam who amuses himself by referring to the Dutch in Holland as "cloggies," not least because a goodly number are racially prejudiced toward him and his children there and have badly beaten up one of his sons). Predictably—in view of the history—there are still places in South Africa that are toy-town Holland out in the African Bush, even though Holland officially washed its hands of its Afrikaner cousins in the days of apartheid.

There are white Dutch-Afrikaners today who are unable to leave the past behind them and who leave the country because they can no longer stand it in South Africa with the blacks in control now or because they cannot find decent or superior jobs there, as before, with good prospects. For all of this, they blame the ANC and the way in which it has taken over from the past, with its Black Economic Empowerment (BEE) policies that have inevitably done them out of many of the top jobs that formerly fell so effortlessly into their laps.

I am mostly talking about white Dutch-Afrikaners in South Africa—not white others—because there are big religious and racial difference between the Dutch and other white Afrikaners. According to the late Heidi Holland, a half-British half-Swiss freelance journalist (with a Dutch surname!) who died mysteriously in South Africa in August in 2012, "[we] whites are undoubtedly in denial about the damage inflicted by us on black South Africans," and she reckoned that they will be in denial for decades to come, in what is "arguably the most complicated society on earth."

The complications are racial, psychological, emotional, and social, all intertwined with the historical and political fabric of South Africa today. No wonder many South Africa watchers in Britain and the West cannot work it all out—a lot of people inside South Africa cannot disentangle it in their hearts and minds either. It is a confusing and confused situation. The fact that the late Nelson Mandela and his successors managed to defuse and contain it for some two decades now is greatly to their credit, much more to their credit than to the credit of many white racists and former racists who have been sufficiently off the radar, thus far, not to make a difference for the worse.

But in order to defuse a situation, one needs to analyze, clarify, and articulate it to control it, not to go into denial about it and sweep it under the carpet—hence this book by one who really wants to see South Africa succeed as a multiracial and multicultural, peaceful nation, in the best traditions of Nelson Mandela. But not without doing something substantial for the black underclass there, which cannot be taken for granted forever (just as in Victorian Britain, the white underclass in their Dickensian slums could not be ignored at length). I have always wanted this for South Africa from the 1960s when I first gave moral support to the anti-apartheid movement in London and for the release of Nelson Mandela. And here I am, in my seventy-fourth year, still standing on many of my 1960s principles and beliefs to this day. I still believe that the nation can work if only people will listen to reason and shed their racist skins—but there's the rub, because they may not do so, given that some of these psychological complications mentioned by Heidi Holland before she died have morphed so deeply into such headstrong denial that they have become invisible.

If one deeply denies that such complications exist, or that one's racist attitude and color prejudice still exists in the post-apartheid years, then for all intents and purposes, they no longer exist in one's consciousness, and are no longer visible to oneself when they are very visible to everybody else! Such complications and prejudices have been miraculously white-washed out of one's head! But one does not usually get this impression from visits to South Africa that last a couple of weeks or more, for holiday or business purposes, and this is either because there is no time for keen observation, or because visitors' minds are on other more pleasurable things.

One cannot get under the skin of a place and its people in a couple of weeks—a longer period of time is required, as are many more visits, conversations, or even arguments with the locals along these lines. One cannot get any of this from conversations about golf, the excellence of South Africa's world-class golf clubs, rugby, cricket, and South Africa's other sporting life, its superb shopping malls, its breathtaking landscape, or its garden route for tourists—in short, its wild life rather than its human interracial life. Because there is precious little cultural life in South Africa—culture doesn't interest most whites and others there (Afrikaners and others), most of whom are interested in more practical and sporty things than cultural or intellectual things, with too few art galleries, libraries, museums, and stage theaters of any note—there is precious little cultural or intellectual talk, let alone interracial psychological talk.

What one gets, instead, is polite conversation about nothing or very little in particular, and certainly not about racially or psychologically sensitive issues if they can possibly be avoided, as they usually can. Whatever else may be said about white Dutch-Afrikaner and other white racists in South Africa today, one cannot say they are not polite. They are politely very racist and everything else you care to mention! Their politeness is like a religion to them—unless you come across them out in the bush, where there are a lot white Zulus waving their spears and beating their shields! While there is some occasional political talk against the ANC—noticeably in white homes behind locked doors—that is let slip from time to time, there is not much of that either in the late Heidi Holland's "most complicated society on earth." That is also one of the most polite societies on earth, with so much sanitized and polite conversation, that there is never any knowing what people think, or if they actually do "think" at all!

Whatever it is, they are not going to tell you, and whatever they think about you is going to be said behind your back, which is the norm there—much more than elsewhere and certainly more than in Britain—so you will seldom know where you stand. A Belgian-Afrikaner I know, who is in business there, tells me, "We can never get our clients to tell us what they think of our service, or if or how it can be improved. We ask them all the time, but they don't tell us, and they don't respond to surveys or questionnaires. So we never know if and where we went wrong or are going wrong, or what we can do to improve our service or learn from our mistakes. If and when we lose a client, we never know why, because when we ask them, they are too polite to tell us!"

His Jewish-Afrikaner partner agrees. Not that these two are short of clients, I am glad to say, because they run an excellent business that offers a very good service indeed, but they are open-minded and self-confident enough to discuss these matters, just as most businesses in Britain and the West would do. If you are going to South Africa for business reasons, you can make a note of this. Many of your white clients or bosses will politely smile in your direction while getting rid of you behind your back. There is a kind of formal politeness in South Africa that means approximately nothing and is, for sure, very sickly sweet indeed for those with a sweet tooth for it! People don't like to admit to anything bad or have an embarrassing or ugly scene. They prefer to smile sweetly and move on, keeping their own ugly secrets.

There is a kind of peekaboo psychological game going on in which one moment you see what people are thinking and where they stand, and the next moment you don't, when the lace curtains in their heads are drawn.

It's as if they are brought up to believe that it's always best not to let people know where they stand or what they think, especially if they are not your kind of people; it's as if they are brought up to believe that it's rude to let people know that you are not happy with them or the service that they have to offer.

One is reminded of "polite society" in England's early-nineteenth-century Regency days of Jane Austen, who wrote the novel *Pride and Prejudice* in 1813, when it was not considered polite conversation to discuss all manner of uncomfortable or potentially embarrassing things that nevertheless needed to be aired! So all societies have been there and done that, but the snail's pace white South Africans are still back there in the early nineteenth century in these respects, not in today's twenty-first century! Too many of their white women put one in mind of the Jane Austen era—only the dress is different, not the quaint and ornamental manners.

There are all sorts of taboo subjects in white South African society that are not considered to be "nice"—such as sex, homosexuality, atheism, swearing, and apartheid—that are not infrequently out of conversational bounds, as I have noticed on my visits over the years. The white women who don't like what they hear will often quite unexpectedly leave the room or otherwise storm out of it, and even burst into tears about! In some families, women are not infrequently kept in a sexual apartheid of their own by their men, who will wait until the women have left the room before talking "man's talk" behind the backs of their women (not that their women always seem to mind this; in fact some actually seem to prefer it).

But what are not taboo subjects for white men and women equally, in the company of each other in their homes, are stories about how awful President Zuma and his black policemen are, and how Zuma will plunge the country into misery and chaos before long. Stories of the alleged corruption and stupidity of Zuma and his black policemen are gleefully popular in anti-ANC white homes, and I was amused to find, on one occasion, that when a mildly racist, younger white Afrikaner male I know crashed his car into the back of another driver and was treated well by the black police after he had disrespected them, neither he nor his family wanted to admit that he had been treated well.

Because he had been racially dismissive of and offhand with the black police that were called to the scene of his road accident, belittling them when they arrived, as if they were of no consequence, and refusing to cooperate with them with his white nose high in the air—they very reasonably decided to teach him a lesson, but in the nicest possible way!

They could have arrested him on the spot, but they elected instead to detain him in their police station, where they would not release him until he had cleaned one of their police cars by hand in order to teach him "how to be respectful to black policemen" and not to lie to them!

He had lied to them about not having his ID card with him when they asked to see it.

Clearly the black policemen's treatment of him was a lot better than his being arrested for rudely disrespecting them, and better by far than being locked up in a prison cell or worse. As we have seen already in this book, the white Dutch-Afrikaner police, in the days of apartheid, stripped Steve Biko naked and tortured him to death for twenty-two hours.

What had happened to him was this: when the police arrived on the scene and asked to see his driving license and ID (one is required to carry ID cards at all times in South Africa), he dismissively told them that he had left his documentation at home, which was not true, because he had his ID with him, but couldn't be bothered to show it. No doubt he gave the impression that he thought them impertinent fools and did his best to trivialize them in his usual way. Probably he was annoyed with the driver in front of him for suddenly braking and causing the crash in the first place (unless he was driving too close from behind), and he was almost certainly additionally annoyed to be asked questions by mere black policemen who had the "impertinence" and "temerity" to question him at all.

But when the black policemen searched his car—always on the lookout for drugs or guns—they discovered that he did indeed have his ID with him, contrary to what he had told them, and when they confronted him with this lie, he did not apologize, but continued to treat them as if they were of no consequence, petulant and headstrong young fellow that he is. Which was when they told him that they were taking him back to the police station with them to teach him how to respect black policemen!

If this infuriated him to begin with, on second thought it soon alarmed him (who knows what they might do to him?), so he immediately got on his cell phone to his mother, who became even more alarmed than he was. She, in turn, phoned her daughter, who joined the chorus of alarm and immediately went with her husband in their car to the police station in question, to see what had become of her brother, fearing the worst! Had the black policemen beaten him up and chucked him in a ditch? What had they done to him to "teach him a lesson?" But all they had done was made him clean a police car! They had given him a bucket of water and a cloth and said something like "go clean that car over there and make a good job of it, you disrespectful young white racist puppy dog"—or words to that effect—"and when you have finished it we'll come back and inspect it to make sure that you have done a good job."

When his sister and her white husband—his brother-in-law—arrived, his sister was not amused, but his brother-in-law (who was English) could not keep a straight face. Consider yourself lucky, he told the young white racist, that this is all they are doing to you—it's like being back at school again, or in the army, and given a chore by the headmaster or sergeant to punish you kindly for your stupid offences and your unco-operative and ungentlemanly behavior. Why so uncoopera-tive? They could have locked you up in a cell, charged you, or physically abused you when nobody was looking.

This wise and non-racist brother-in-law politely asked the police if he could help clean the car to save time—by cleaning the inside while the disrespectful young Afrikaner man cleaned the outside—to which they readily agreed. When the job was done, they inspected the car inside and out and then released their prisoner with a mere caution, which was "don't lie to or disrespect the police in future, and remember to carry your driving license and insurance with you at all times. Don't push your luck with the police in future."

But did this young white racist, with his disdain for black policemen, consider himself lucky on this occasion? Not a bit of it. He insulted the police (behind their backs this time) even more for daring to make him clean their car and wasting his time. The moral of this story is so obvious that it hardly needs to be stated, but I will state it just the same, in case anybody wants to overlook or dispute it: do not refuse to cooperate with black policemen in South Africa just because they are black!

So, as we see, not all black South African policemen are bad. On the contrary, they may only be partly bad or not bad at all, like all policemen all over the world, whatever their skin color. But this story of how lenient and philosophically clever—and also non-racist and helpful—black policemen can be in South Africa today is not the kind of story that you will hear told in most white Afrikaner homes, where this kind of thing is best forgotten and swiftly swept under the rug. Nor is it the kind of story that would be interpreted in this way, as I am interpreting it here. On the contrary, it would be taken as further evidence of the racist impertinence of these blacks, racially humiliating a white man by making him clean one of their police cars for their own amusement. How dare they! See how bad things are becoming in President Zuma's South Africa? The way things are going, they will soon be required to pay their black cleaners, gardeners, and other menials an honest day's pay for an honest day's work (President Zuma has already observed that they might consider doing this)! Before long, there will be a basic minimum wage, *mein gott*! What is the black world coming to? Things were never this bad under apartheid.

A German-Scottish Afrikaner young woman told me on a recent visit to South Africa, "The reason why a lot of white

South Africans do not welcome open and frank conversation about sensitive, controversial, or debatable matters is because they think they are being judged by others." One could add to this that maybe they have too much to be judged for or too much to hide, and not least from themselves. It was her German-Afrikaner mother who once told me that the Jewish Holocaust was a myth created as propaganda by the British against the Germans during World War II!

If all you want to do is to talk business and about making money (both excellent subjects, if you ask me), play golf, swim in the pool, and enjoy a garden party, then white South Africa is a great place to be, but not otherwise, because too many people's minds and conversations are closed, or otherwise programmed about what they can or cannot say at any given time or place and in whose company, and how much of the truth it is "polite" to discuss. I even know white Christian fundamentalists in South Africa who forbid you to take the Lord's name in vain in their homes. They will also expect you to pray and bless the Lord for the food before eating it! And as for honest and racially unprejudiced political talk about President Zuma and the ANC, forget it! These are the kind of white people who will never vote for the ANC or almost any black political candidate.

As we see, we have more genre pictures in this chapter with which to enrich and shed more light on our story. But the overall picture and situation strikes me as being hugely absurd and absurdly complicated, as the late Heidi Holland has correctly suggested, not least because of all this psychological trickery and dishonesty and its emotionally racist complications; not to mention all the interracial rivalries, histories, jealousies, resentments, mistrusts, and occasional hates between the Dutch, British, Portuguese, Greek, Italian, Huguenot, and other white tribes in South Africa today—as they all make their two-faced efforts to be friendly and "nice" to and with each other—and never mind the blacks, Jews, and Indians, and that's even before one comes to consider the intertribal rivalries between the blacks.

Yet there are white exceptions to this general rule—as there are always exceptions. I am reminded of an Italian-Afrikaner restaurateur I know in South Africa who says that he regards his black headwaiter as a brother, and I do believe that he does, given that he said this in front of the smiling black waiter with an arm round his shoulder. I got to know the waiter rather well in the Italian-Afrikaner's absence when I invited him to take a drink at my table, and he did not strike me as being the kind of man who was scared to speak his thought about his boss, or anybody else for that matter.

Heidi Holland referred to this racial "complication" in South Africa (which she did not explore and explain, as I am attempting to do here) in a column for *The Star* newspaper entitled "A Disservice to White Citizens" on May 21st, 2009, in which she invited whites to consider if more humility and apology was required from them for their sorry history and their present-day attitudes, and even for their whiteness (in terms of their whiter-than-white frame of mind). Certainly the young white Afrikaner I have described who chose not to cooperate with the black police could have done with much more humility (I doubt that the word is even in his vocabulary).

If any white journalist was fair to President Zuma, it was certainly Heidi Holland, not that this got her anywhere with her own white community. She suggested that Helen Zille—the German-Jewish-Afrikaner leader of the Democratic Alliance, which is the white opposition party in South Africa—was performing a "disservice to whites" by performing what Heidi obviously considered to be her racially prejudiced behavior against President Zuma in her criticisms of him. Heidi even suggested that the Democratic Alliance leader "might profitably be offered time off for a nervous breakdown," in view of her attack on Zuma and the touchy feelings that Heidi reckoned that she had about him for his sexual and other attitudes to which we shall come in the following chapter. Needless to say, Heidi Holland was hardly ever popular with too many white Dutch-Afrikaners, but she did have a big following among non-racist white others and also blacks.

Comparing white South Africa to post–World War II Germany, she pointed out the racial trauma that both communities had in common. It is no doubt true that those who have committed horrendous sins and crimes not infrequently go into denial afterwards in order to be able to live with themselves. This is, unless they are extraordinarily honest and mature people, able either to live with what they or their parents and grandparents have done, for whatever reason, or otherwise to forget it and repent it (learning from their truthfully confessed mistakes in the process), because there really is nothing else they can do about it anymore—where else can they go, if not into denial?

But unless those in denial do learn from their mistakes, they will of course carry on making the same old racist (and other) mistakes, time and again, because they will still be stuck in their unrepentant, shameless past with an accompanying mind-set, as many are in white South Africa, even though time has moved them on into the present and the future (*time* has moved *them* on, even though they have not *moved themselves* on). Because there is no halfway decent reason why today's young white generations in South Africa should be blamed for the sins of their fathers and grandfathers—that is not the way of the civilized world, and three cheers for Nelson Mandela for recognizing this—we all have to move on from whatever kind of past that haunts or condemns us. There would be absolutely no hope otherwise. We would live in an endless cycle of ferocious revenge upon revenge and hatred upon hatred handed down from one generation to the next. But this doesn't mean that we have to forgive the past necessarily. We just have to learn how to live with it and not lose too much sleep over bad things about which nothing very much can be done anymore, and to concentrate instead on the present and the future in order to make sure that these things are not repeated, that we do not return to the past in the present.

Quoting the twentieth-century and Nobel and Pulitzer Prize–winning American novelist William Faulkner, Heidi Holland reminded us that the past is never dead and that few of us are ever (or let us say hardly ever) past the past. This is true of different people, to a greater or lesser extent, and it is also an interesting and compelling thing about the past and our history. Our history is too important to be swept under the rug where we cannot learn anything from it. Because the past dictates our present and future—to whichever extent it does— how we are today and what we can expect of ourselves and others today and tomorrow is not infrequently decided by our and their history, unless we manage to put our history behind us (but even then, not without difficulty). How others behave and how we feel about their behavior—and how we think they should behave—is also conditioned by our history as well as our present-day experiences. It is our evolving history that dictates the kind of people we are or think that we are, and how we think and behave in consequence, and the extent to which we have a sympathetic sense of fair play.

But we need to know our history in the first place if we are to be changed for the better by it and if we are to be troubled by our conscience over bad deeds in the past. But if we don't know the history, then the past does not touch us and we do not understand how it is in any way relevant. If we cannot face up to our past and be content with or proud of it, then our behavior is always going to be mentally and emotionally subversive as we deny all sorts of things about it—or are genuinely ignorant of it. If we cannot face up to our past and live with it without shame because it really was too shameful, then our behavior is always going to be problematic, and not least for others who have to deal with and accommodate us.

Some in Britain say that it takes three generations to make a gentleman from a peasant or working-class family, but in the case of South Africa, the question is how many generations does it take to turn white racists inside out so that they are not racists anymore? More than three generations? Another apt saying is that one can take the person out of the slum, but not the slum out of the person, and again, in the context of South Africa, the question for Dutch-Afrikaners is how long does it take to take their racially prejudiced slum mentalities out of them?

The younger generation of Dutch and other Afrikaners have, quite rightly, been given the benefit of the doubt about not being racist anymore, and in my experience this is probably true of those who really have moved on and come clean about what was wrong with their racism and needed to be put right. But it is obviously not true of less honest and less mature others who have gone into denial instead of coming clean. For all these reasons and more, white racism against blacks does seem to be alive and well in South Africa still—albeit much more understated than before, as you might expect—but with the possible exception of, in my experience, the very professional business, international, and other sectors, where intelligent business minds are quick to see what is good and bad business, and to avoid racial prejudice and racially prejudiced minds like the plague!

But how's this for even more astonishingly incredible Dutch-Afrikaner attitudes to their Dutch cousins in faraway Holland in Northern Europe (many of whom in Amsterdam tell me that they refer to their South African Afrikaner cousins as "retards"!)? Many Dutch-Afrikaners actually think that they have something to forgive Holland for letting their Dutch-Afrikaner cousins down and not supporting them in the days of apartheid! Not that they have any intention of forgiving the Dutch in Holland for this.

In the June 2010 edition of the *Wall Street Journal*, a confused article entitled "South Africa Forgives the Dutch: A Nation Whose Colonists Brought Apartheid, Wins Eager Applause on the Pitch," referred to the 2010 World Cup that was staged in South Africa.

This article implied that because a handful of black and white South Africans were applauding Holland's soccer team and cheering it on, it followed from this that South African blacks had forgiven the Dutch for imposing apartheid and colonialism on them, while white Dutch-Afrikaners had forgiven the Dutch for not having stood by them during the apartheid era.

As we have seen from my Zulu taxi driver in the previous chapter, many blacks will never forgive the Dutch-Afrikaners, whom they believe will have to get down on their knees before God if they are to be forgiven! But, according to the article, "African blacks whose long history of oppression . . . came largely at the hands of the Dutch settlers and their descendants" and endured "the indignity that dark-skinned South Africans suffered at the hands of the Dutch-speaking oppressors" —(true)—"no longer regard Holland primarily as the perpetrators" (the article couldn't be more wrong about this!). Many South African blacks certainly do still regard the Dutch and their Dutch-Afrikaner cousins as the perpetrators because they are not so ignorant of their history, but they have moved on, for all that, and they know that it is the Dutch-Afrikaners they have to forgive, not latter-day Holland that never supported these Afrikaners in the first place and was always opposed to apartheid (except for the Dutch Reform Church).

At least one reader, Pieter Du Preeze, emailed the paper to say he had "no affinity with the Netherlands," and this is also my experience of both South African blacks and Dutch-Afrikaner whites generally—they appear not to have an affinity with or liking for Holland, the land of their former colonizers, much less have forgiven Holland for whatever it is that the *Wall Street Journal* imagines they have to forgive it for, just because they like its soccer team! But the *Wall Street Journal* touched a nerve in white South Africa's Dutch-Afrikaner community for all that, because, in my experience, it generally does think that it has something to forgive Holland for: having cold-shouldered it in the days of apartheid, when the

Dutch-Afrikaners were in their own estimation being proudly Dutch (and German).

Most South African blacks have an affinity with Britain, for all the reasons explained hitherto in these pages, but not usually with Holland (not that this prevented Nelson Mandela going to Holland and healing wounds there), and hardly any whites that I come across have a declared affinity with Holland. Holland's black soccer legend, Ruud Gullit, dedicated his Footballer of the Year Award to Nelson Mandela back in 1987, and the following year he recorded an anti-apartheid song entitled "South Africa" with the reggae band Revelation Time as a political statement in favor of black South Africa (note that Gullit is a black, not white, Dutch soccer player).

Most black South Africans that I have spoken to were supporting Ghana after their own team was knocked out of the World Cup, not Holland, but I do not doubt that a small percentage of white Dutch-Afrikaners were supporting Holland, but certainly not most blacks, for the historical reasons already explained in this book. If a few blacks were supporting Holland—and one black supporter of Holland was quoted in the *Wall Street Journal* article—then it testifies to the progress that the truth, reconciliation, and forgiveness programs have made, and this is very much to the credit of Nelson Mandela and South African blacks, but I doubt that many blacks or indeed white Dutch-Afrikaner whites have suddenly "forgiven" Holland, as the article suggested.

Without doubt the big racial and political mess that was made in South Africa after the British left in 1948—one that remained until 1994—was a Dutch-Afrikaner mess that goes all the way back to the seventeenth-century Dutch of colonial history. It was a mess that was characteristically, culturally, and historically Dutch—not British or French Huguenot (the latter never had the power to do very much about it either way)—but it was closer to the fascist traditions of the Germans under Hitler during World War II, than it was close to latter-day postwar Holland.

Not that it matters anymore to the outside world—if it ever did in the first place—whether South African blacks and whites have or have not forgiven the Dutch in Holland. What matters from here on is whether they have truly forgiven each other.

When a writer—or any visual artist for that matter—holds a mirror up to society, he or she finds his or her own reflection in that mirror, as well as all the other reflections, and if he or she is honest, such writers or visual artists do not attempt to disguise this or to hide their own hand in the way in which they portray, reveal, and interpret the reflections. Their opinions and ideas will be all part of the thought-provoking picture—especially if they have plenty of relevant experience of the matters in question—and it is for viewers to make up their own minds about what has been depicted and how in the two-way mirror between artists or viewers. The joy of reading and thinking is entirely due to the two-way nature of the mirror: looking at reflections in different ways and deciding how you choose to look at them and why. Viewers are free to make up their own minds and draw their own conclusions, regardless of the conclusions in the picture that are suggested to them in order to provoke thought, not to tell them how to think, which is entirely their own affair.

While this stands to reason, it is, alas, not always remembered by viewers who either flee from the mirror in horror or become so annoyed by it that they try to smash it! When it comes to racially divided South Africa, there are a lot of racial and historical complications to think about, as Heidi Holland has usefully reminded us, and to look at from different angles.

While this concept of viewing is usually but not entirely more applicable to works of factually based nonfiction than it is to works of fiction that are purely imaginative—and generally more concerned with the imagination therefore than with debatable matters of political, racial, and historical fact—there are some borderline cases even in works of fiction. In South Africa, it seems to me that the relationship between fact and fiction in the minds of the racially divided communities there and what they think about each other—and of the local white journalists and authors who write about all this—is too often blurred in so-called factual thinking, writing, and policy making.

Is it a fact or a fiction that the blacks really have forgiven the whites to whom they became reconciled under Nelson Mandela; that the whites are no longer racist toward blacks, or are they as racist (secretly) as they ever were; that South Africa has forgiven Holland and has something to forgive it for; that the country is as racially complicated as Heidi Holland has suggested; that President Zuma is a rapist, as alleged (see chapters nine and ten), and is secretly trying to put the clock back by interfering behind the scenes with South Africa's laws and its freedom of expression?

As we see, there is a lot to distinguish and to clarify between fact and fiction in South Africa today, which is of course why Heidi Holland said that it is the most complicated country on earth (and complicated by its own hand and of its own making, one might add).

CHAPTER EIGHT

The Mysterious Death of Heidi Holland

A WORD ABOUT the aforesaid Heidi Holland, quoted in the previous chapter, who mysteriously died in Johannesburg in 2012. It is a fact that she died, but at the time of writing, we still do not know the facts of her death. A doctor or some doctors know these facts, but they have not come forward about them.

She is already sadly missed by a great many who admired her journalism campaign for a more racially harmonious and liberated South Africa and for less racial prejudice in the white community. She was an occasional friend of Nelson Mandela's and had her photograph taken with him, which appeared in some of her obituaries in the press in London, and now Nelson has also died this year, a year after Heidi.

She was also said to be in close touch, off-record, with British diplomats behind the scenes, whom she wanted to get together with the president of Zimbabwe, Robert Mugabe, unofficially, with a view to getting Britain and Zimbabwe back together. But this doesn't mean that she had no qualms about Mugabe, only that she had qualms about the ongoing rift between Britain and Zimbabwe that she thought was in neither side's interest and was therefore worth healing, if a way could be found. This would not have made her popular with Mugabe's black political opponents and victims in Zimbabwe. Nor would it have made her popular with whites in South Africa to whom, predictably, Mugabe is anathema, as well as to a goodly number of perfectly ordinary Zimbabwean blacks among whom Heidi's book on Mugabe may have been seen as a betrayal. So there were plenty of people who had it in for Heidi Holland when she died in mysterious circumstances in South Africa.

While she was almost certainly hopelessly wrong about mending the rift with Mugabe, this didn't make her wrong about everything else that she thought. But we shall never know how wrong she may have been because the British government was having nothing to do with her proposal, even though its diplomats were apparently speaking off-record with her to see whether to go with it or not, and now that she is dead, both the European Union and Britain are speaking to Mugabe again! One says that British diplomats were "apparently" lending an ear to her because one can never be entirely sure what diplomats are doing with their slippery ears and tongues.

Heidi had written an empathic and sympathetic biography of Robert Mugabe, who had granted her a two and a half hour interview in Harare for the purpose, because he considered her sufficiently non-racist for him to get a fair hearing. According to *The Economist*'s obituary of Heidi in August 2012, this was "the best biography to date on Zimbabwe's despotic leader." *The Economist* also said of her that "few other independent journalists have achieved quite so much by sheer drive, wit, and charm." I, for one, can testify from my own globe-trotting that this is what it takes. It also takes bravery, of which Heidi had plenty.

For example, while Heidi was a friend of the ANC, she nevertheless saw fit to criticize it for the alleged corruption and mismanagement of which it had been publicly accused, just as she had also publicly accused South African whites and the Democratic Alliance of being too white in more ways than one and thereby too racist for their own good.

So she had become a thorn in the flesh of both sides, albeit much more so in the flesh of the white side.

I am devoting this chapter to Heidi not just because the evidence suggests that she was by far the most outstanding, thought-provoking, anti-racist, and anti–white supremacist journalist and campaigner in South Africa, but also because of the unsatisfactory mystery surrounding her death that remains to be resolved and deserves therefore to be put on record in these pages. If this book can break the wall of silence about Heidi Holland and get to the bottom of her mysterious death, so much the better.

She was very much a part of the Nelson Mandela, President Zuma, and South Africa story in which her voice became prominent, as she played a leading role where racial tensions are concerned. In a way, it looks like Heidi Holland was a "tranquil oasis" in the midst of a desert of arid and unproductive racial despair, with the whites on one side of the vast expanse, psychologically speaking, and the blacks on the other. But Heidi certainly crossed that expanse of this psychological desert in her writing. Heidi Holland lived in Johannesburg, where she had been born in 1947, one year before apartheid in South Africa in 1948, before her parents moved to Rhodesia (not Zimbabwe in those days), when she was three. She finished running her own guest house in the trendy suburb of Melville in Johannesburg much later on in her life before finally dying there in 2012. Her British-Swiss parents probably got out of Johannesburg because they did not like the new Dutch-Afrikaner nationalism and apartheid government there that succeeded the departure of the British.

Heidi's view was that journalists and other writers should avoid being dispassionate in the service of their moral and ethical objectives—that they absolutely should have such objectives!—and that in South Africa, peace and stability could not be taken for granted because they were more precarious than they appeared to be on the surface. She had personal experience of this because she had twice been violently attacked by black criminals in Johannesburg, who knew nothing of her mission to achieve greater racial harmony in South Africa as well as less white prejudice against blacks, and also because some whites there who detested her for her pro-black racial and political opinions. For this and so many other reasons, she feared that the deep wounds in South African society were not healing as intended by the late Nelson Mandela.

In my view they certainly are healing, albeit slowly, but it will take time, much more time yet, and in the meantime, people are of course at risk from the black criminals in their midst—and from white assassins, if they are black politicians! I take the view that there is no "quick fix" for a recovery from apartheid, but the fix that we have so far is surviving pretty well. If people really want it, it will become a permanent fix, but all sides will have to work at it, and if they do not do so for some crazy reason best known to themselves, then things will no doubt fall apart. My reading of Heidi was that she was telling whites to lay off Zuma and give the man a chance.

It's a great pity that Heidi did not write a book about Nelson Mandela or Jacob Zuma, and, had she lived longer, maybe she would have done so—I cannot say because I never knew her.

When an author writes about people he or she does not or has not known personally, as I am doing in this book where the lead players are concerned, if he or she is any good, he or she probably writes a more investigative and informed book than books that are written about the people in question by their friends or people who knew them. This is because he or she can be more objective and detached and won't be afraid of disappointing or offending the book subject.

For this reason, I generally prefer books about people that are not written by those that knew or know them, because they are likely to be more detached and not so narrowly focused, especially when written by authors who know their subject well and have covered the ground well (in this case South Africa and its politics, people, and history, all of which are no less important than the famous and other people in question), which is why—in the right hands—one can learn more from these more detached books than those written by their friends, colleagues, or indeed by themselves in their autobiographies. As for books that are ghostwritten for famous and other people, it stands to reason that the ghostwriters' strings are being pulled by their clients. Readers are well advised to bear all these things in mind when reading biographical and auto-biographical books.

The trouble with books written by authors about people they know is that too many of these authors behave as if they "own" the people they know and that only they can write about them, which is not only absurd but also very far from the truth. Once people become public figures or celebrities, with their distinct public personas, there is nothing private about them anymore, and there is no reason why authors who have studied their personas and its impact on their fans, but do not know them personally, cannot write about them as well as anybody else. Heidi Holland was a twice-married single mom and freelance journalist with a regular column in South Africa's *Star* newspaper. She had several books to her credit, with much more writing in her by all accounts, but her life was cut short when she died suddenly and prematurely at sixty-four years of age on August 14, 2012, when the *Daily Telegraph* in London told us in an obituary that "her family said she took her own life."

No other newspaper seems to have reported this or anything else as the cause of her death, and it was extraordinary that she should have suddenly taken it into her head to do such a thing.

But the *Telegraph* did not tell us why, or if she left a suicide note. The plot thickened when the ANC government and Democratic Alliance opposition party in South Africa reported her death but also without saying what she died of, and this again was mysterious.

What could have been so possibly shameful or embarrassing about her death? Why could the South African and British publics not be allowed to know? Why did the South African media not demand to know? Do the British and Dutch embassies and their diplomats know? If not, why not, and if so, why are they so tight-lipped? Heidi wasn't HIV-positive, was she? (I jest, of course, and let's not forget that she was supposed to have had a great sense of humor.)

One presumes and hopes that she was not HIV-positive, given that she had attacked Helen Zille of the Democratic Alliance Party for calling President Zuma a "self-confessed womanizer with sexist views who puts his wives at risk by having unprotected sex with an HIV-positive woman." Heidi's reply to this was that Zille "should have demonstrated a rare political humility by apologizing," and she asked if Zille he had "forgotten that disdain for the dignity of others gives impetus to rampant nationalism. Surely apartheid taught us that?" All this and more was published in the South African press as well as broadcast on Radio Netherlands.

What we were originally told of Heidi Holland's death— from friends and close colleagues, as well as news reports— was that she was on antibiotics prescribed by her doctor in Johannesburg for a stomach complaint and that she reportedly dropped dead (unless she was struck dead) in her garage and was found there by neighbors. And so her life ended as controversially as this compassionate and anti-racism woman had lived it, with so much empathy for blacks on whose behalf she was shocked by the white racism against them. She also lived with a fair amount of secrecy along the way, just as secrecy has surrounded the cause or possible causes of her death and the reasons for it. Was it really suicide? Why would she take her own life? Why is nobody asking more questions? Her white Afrikaner critics have written her off as being too "starry eyed" about blacks, but they seem to see no contradiction in their being too "starry-eyed" about whites and their white politics in contrast to black politics.

The secrecy in Heidi's life came chiefly from her off-record meetings with British diplomats whom she is supposed to have advised (they will deny it, of course)—in her Johannesburg guesthouse—on the subject of Mugabe, his state of mind, and how best to deal with him. But David Miliband, Britain's foreign secretary in the New Labor government of Gordon Brown (2007–2010), is reportedly said to have dismissed her idea of a behind-the-scenes approach to President Mugabe as off the wall, not only on the grounds that Mugabe is an undesirable, but also because Heidi was suggesting eighty-six-year-old Lady Soames as a go-between, the widow of Britain's last governor in Rhodesia!

There is, as far as I know, no evidence for any of this, but these are the unsubstantiated reports that have been circulating about Heidi and her contact with the British government. It would be a very easy thing for New Labor to substantiate these reports, or otherwise, by releasing the necessary documentation. All sorts of speculative and highly fanciful rumors circulated about the possible cause of Heidi Holland's death when she died—but not suicide, as suggested in the *Daily Telegraph* (she had no known record of depression previously). These rumors ranged from murder by a burglar who broke into her home, poison from a secret agent in the event of Heidi having discovered something that a government or political party was trying to cover up, and an incurable illness that she hadn't told anyone about, to some kind of accident maybe. The ANC and Democratic Alliance didn't help in demystifying any of this, by not showing their hand and explaining all; unless they explained and then persuaded the South African press not to publish because of the embarrassing nature of the cause of her death.

If we are to believe what her family has reportedly told to the *Daily Telegraph*—that she committed suicide—that is certainly surprising, but nonetheless mysterious.

Why would she—why did she? Heidi really did die as controversially and mysteriously as she lived, and no doubt this, at least, would have pleased her!

After her birth in 1944, when she had been taken by her parents to live in Ian Smith's Rhodesia/Robert Mugabe's Zimbabwe, she had attended the Ellis Robins School in Salisbury, a city in which she started her career in journalism at a magazine there called *Illustrated Life Rhodesia*. When she eventually got back to South Africa decades later, her guesthouse in the Johannesburg suburb of Melville reportedly became a meeting place and regular haunt for journalists, activists, aid workers, think tankers, academics, intellectuals, diplomats, and so on, who either stayed or met there. Because she had her fingers in so many pies, there was never any knowing what she may have been up to next, or what may have happened next, but we do know that she was writing a book on the subject of (and against) racism when she suddenly and unexpectedly died.

While she had many foes and naysayers in the white Afrikaner community who criticized her and her work, as a result of her criticism of the racial prejudices of which she relentlessly accused them, she had her admirers also, and it is hard to know if she had black enemies in Zimbabwe for being too kind or too partial to Robert Mugabe in their view. Let's not forget that Mahatma Gandhi was killed in India by a fellow Hindu for being too partial to Muslims—he who had worked as a lawyer in South Africa where there is a settlement and museum in his honor to this day in Phoenix just outside Durban—so such motivations are not unheard of.

She reportedly liked to call women "doll," "dollface," and "sugar lips" in her home and at social and other gatherings—regardless of their exalted rank—and she was reckoned to have been as open and chatty about some things as she was secretive about others (such as the secret diplomacy that she practiced, without being a spy, presumably, and about her health problem for which she was on antibiotics just before she died). Her doctor will know what she died of, but like everyone else, he is not saying.

She is said to have had a legendary, sharp-edged tongue, as sharp as her wit, to go with her great sense of humor, and by all accounts she gave no outward signs to anybody that she was dying or might be dying, and given her journalistic belief in transparency, one would have expected her to be transparent about any serious illness or disease that she may have had. As I say, all very mysterious indeed.

CHAPTER NINE

Citizen Number One or Enemy of the People?

Wʜᴇɴ ᴛʜᴇ Mᴀʀɪᴋᴀɴᴀ miners' strike at the Lonmin mine near Rustenburg hit the headlines and television screens in South Africa and the outside world in September 2012, the well-known political and racist enemies of both the ANC and President Zuma were stupidly rejoicing and no doubt hoping to dance on either or both's political grave by falsely accusing him of introducing a police state and by trying to get everybody worried about it.

This strike and Zuma's alleged overreaction to it was a stark reminder, his enemies suggested, of his bad and hasty decision making and the ANC's inability to govern without bloodshed and government-sponsored violence (never mind that there had been no government violence or bloodshed for almost twenty years previously). But what to expect from a Zulu president, or indeed black miners and the predominantly black ANC?

This was the racially and politically prejudiced misinterpretation put upon this strike and President Zuma's role in it, and it came from his chiefly white Dutch-Afrikaner (and other) enemies in the media in South Africa and also in the United Kingdom.

While not all white Afrikaners are racially and politically prejudiced against President Zuma and the ANC—I know some who are not—too many are, alas, which is sad to see after the greater part of two decades of good and wise ANC leadership and forgiveness for their ghastly past, with or without the alleged corruption that is, as we know, widespread in so many European and other countries of the world. While Zuma's detractors are of course not obliged to be fans of the ANC or its presidents—and are democratically entitled to be critical of it for political reasons of their own—they do themselves no favors by letting their racial prejudice and hysteria get in the way of their political prejudice, using the former to give a push and a shove to the latter, and so they finish up unfairly smearing President Zuma with a view, hopefully in their minds, to discrediting and unseating him.

When some black, trigger-happy South African police who were sent in by President Zuma to quell the Marikana miners' strike suddenly opened fire on the miners on August 16, 2012, thirty-six miners were reportedly shot to death (in the back or otherwise) as a result, as were another two police officers and four unidentified people who somehow got caught up in the shootout, while no less than seventy-eight others (miners and policemen) were injured.

This strike could have been averted for want of an affordable 22 percent salary increase—22 percent of almost nothing, and reportedly a mere two thousand rand overall was finally settled in one payment with the miners in order to get them back to work. What started as a tempest in a teapot finished with a hail of bullets instead, and the rest, as they say, is history; but what to learn from the history?

Very little, if you are racially prejudiced, politically motivated, and tunnel-visioned against President Zuma. That much racial and political prejudice was fired off in the president's direction is what we learn from this, not that the racially prejudiced media that lined up against Zuma and had him in their sights was prepared to admit it. No doubt this was and is what anti-Zuma readers wanted and still want to hear, but perhaps they should consider that, had the police stood back and done nothing, no doubt they and the president would have been criticized and condemned for exactly that, if they had lived to tell the tale. The trigger-happy black police obviously lost their heads and opened fire when the threatening and rampaging miners were all sweeping before them.

But some anti-Zuma white Afrikaner and other journalists in South Africa have used this deeply regrettable incident to suggest that Zuma himself is a trigger-happy Zulu in favor of violence and a police state, and furthermore that he handled this situation badly, ham-fisted black fellow that he is, over-reacting with bullets instead of negotiating with the miners. As we see, Zuma was between a rock and a hard place—whatever he did was not likely to impress. What he and his police did was no more or less than other white leaders have done in their time, in the recent and also the distant past. Yet the impression was given that his behavior was typical black man's behavior, which it manifestly was not.

Remember Sharpeville in 1960, in the bad old days of apartheid? Remember Britain's Margaret Thatcher sending in police from all over the United Kingdom to ferociously fight Arthur Scargill and his miners at the Battle of Cosgrove in Yorkshire in the 1990s and putting the miners behind bars or in the hospital in the process with broken heads and limbs? Remember the white Afrikaner General Jan Smuts crushing a white Afrikaner miners' strike in 1922 at the Rand Mines, when the South Africa Chamber of Mines was in conflict with chiefly white miners who were losing their jobs and being discarded because the price of gold had collapsed?

General Smuts was the white Dutch-Afrikaner Minister of Mines, Interior, and Defense who had already used Imperial troops to sort out a previous strike at the Rand Mines in 1913 where there was much rioting and violence, against which he used his defense forces. In 1922 he declared martial law (as Zuma never did) and sent his white Afrikaner troops in to shoot white miners down and to bomb mixed-race others in South West Africa.

So, as we see, there is nothing specifically black, Zuma-, or Zulu-like about using security forces or violence to put striking miners down, as has been implied by the widespread white South African media and its criticisms of President Zuma's handling of the Marikana strike last year, as if to suggest that it is inconceivable and unheard of in South Africa and elsewhere, as it never was and never is. But if journalists irresponsibly—or deviously or racially—fail to mention this kind of relevant historical context when writing about these distressing and complicated matters, then their readers, who do not know any better, probably think that there is something typically black or Zuma-like and Zulu-like about it.

Against this recent and also distant background of strong-arm tactics used against white miners by white political leaders and security forces in South Africa and the United Kingdom in times past, we see that President Zuma's handling of the miners' strike last year is all of a piece with his historical predecessors and not any better or worse than the rest of them. We see that he is no more trigger-happy than the rest of them. But, being a black Zulu, he has been singled out by his white Afrikaner and other detractors as being potentially or actually more savage, trigger-happy, repressive, and more brutal than the rest. He was described by one white Afrikaner journalist as being responsible for "the most lethal use of force by South African security forces since 1960." By stating the obvious in this meaningless way—the white Dutch-Afrikaner police did indeed shoot down black children as well as adults in the 1960s—the journalist in question conveniently forgot to mention that Zuma did what he had to do, just as Nelson Mandela or Thabo Mbeki would have had to do, just as British and white Dutch Afrikaner leaders have had to do in their time when confronted by violent striking miners. This doesn't mean, of course, that the miners had to be shot to death, that Zuma wanted them shot to death or gave the order for it, or that he made the wrong decision by sending in the police. What it means is that he was badly let down by his police, not that he did not need to send them in.

Zuma's South African and other critics need to make a better case against him than this. South African newspaper readers deserve better. Whites do a disservice to themselves when they go at Zuma thoughtlessly and irrationally.

In the South African media, President Zuma stands widely accused of, among other things, not being a friend of justice, democracy, or the poor people or workers whom he is supposed to represent. As a womanizer and polygamist, he is furthermore accused of committing black women to servitude, not to mention having a child with the underaged girl of a close friend with whom he allegedly did not practice safe sex, and also of raping another woman (one of many alleged sexual exploits besides!). Then there are allegations of corruption that are hurled in his direction.

But the trouble is that none of these rumors or allegations of rape and corruption—or other legal charges that have been brought against him—have been proven and, for sure, some are considerably more debatable, possibly far-fetched, and short of evidence than others.

But the most important thing to say about this is that none of these allegations or charges are proven. Even so, in many white, Indian, and some black minds, the verdict is still out on President Zuma as they wait to see what will come out in the wash in the fullness of time. But thus far, let us repeat that nothing has stuck to him in court. He has walked away a free man and has challenged others to see him in court, others who have backed down.

If President Zuma was in India rather than South Africa— where, in the political classes at the top end of society, it is now a matter of record that a staggering forty members of Parliament have sexually assaulted or raped women, six of whom have been well and truly convicted of rape, while none of the others have been brought to justice—his alleged and spectacularly unproven rape of one woman would not have caused a ripple in the water, never mind a stir, and it has to be noted that it is his white naysayers and political enemies who have stirred this up in South Africa.

While rape is reportedly commonplace out on the streets and in the shantytowns—and gender violence is certainly a problem in the homes—the black political class in South Africa has always striven to set a higher moral tone and standard. This is the morally superior ANC that we are talking about, after all, not India, and not back alleys where the morals of alley cats prevail.

But the allegations don't stop here for Zuma. By the time that nepotism has been added to the list of all the other sins of which he is accused, there is also racketeering, money laundering, and bad political decision making, so there are quite a lot of accusations here for a president in his second term of office—who, as Citizen Number One, is not supposed therefore to be regarded as Public Enemy Number One instead! So which is he?

To judge from his widespread support from millions of black people, they do not consider him to be the enemy of the people; however, an increasing number of whites do and are trying to make this image stick, fearing, no doubt, that he is becoming an enemy of white people. He is accused of not being a friend of whites in South Africa due to some of his observations and criticisms of them, so all things considered, there is a lot of mudslinging and a lot of unsavory food for thought going on here as people come to the conclusion maybe that there's no smoke without a fire. If they are blacks they generally do not—by all accounts not more than a handful do.

The foregoing are all the chief accusations leveled against the president by his detractors in South Africa today—both in the media and in some books about him—but how true are they, and is he as bad as his enemies are characterizing him to be?

In this chapter I shall try to find answers to these questions, which I have discovered are not, as ever, as straightforward as they might sound, given that it is certainly true to say that many of his enemies are not only politically biased against him, but also racially biased as well. This massively clouds and tiresomely confuses and complicates the issue.

In Britain and the rest of the outside world—and not least in the United States that has, for the first time in its history, a black president in his second term of office—South Africa is always of interest for the excellent and truly inspirational example it has set in an otherwise violent and highly volatile, savage, and experimental continent, since the late and masterly Nelson Mandela made his people free, but also racially forgiving.

While so much of Africa has been extremely and consistently bad news, South Africa has generally had good political, economic, commercial, moral, and interracial tidings, and, with common consent, our troubled world needs as much good news as it can get right now. Everything is relative, of course, but in all the above respects, and not least where countering recession is concerned, South Africa has been doing better than most other countries with which it can reasonably be compared and for some two decades now. Fortunes have been and continue to be made there, and capitalism and liberal economics have remained on track, as has the political and moral integrity of the nation, both black and white. While South Africa's mines have been deep in debt, they are not without the natural resources to get out of that debt.

Arguably no other African country—and a goodly number of others besides—has been able to compare with South Africa for the civilized and democratic economic progress that it has made, and it would be reckless of President Zuma indeed to throw all this away, which he doesn't strike one as being unintelligent or reckless enough to do. He has already shown that he is capable of standing up to his violent miners, so there is no reason to suppose that he will not stand up to working-class and trade union others as well, should the need arise. But, at the same time, he is the first president to publicly acknowledge that more needs to be done for the poor and the working classes, so he will stand up for them as well as against them. Clearly, he is not a president to be bullied, but has and always has had an affinity with the poor and the workers that goes way back to his early years, as we have seen in chapter four.

As for his reported desire for a redistribution of wealth—alarming foreign investors and multinational companies as well as the richer South African whites and others, including some of the richer blacks—it can certainly be afforded to some extent, and the sooner we find out to what extent, the better it will be for investor confidence. This President Zuma needs to do now with all possible speed if he is to keep his voters.

Unlike his predecessors, Presidents Mandela and Mbeki, President Zuma has come to power in South Africa positively gift-wrapped with criticisms and allegations, not only from his enemies, but also from some of his black peers in the ANC, who have been opposing him and trying to get rid of him behind the scenes, albeit without success thus far. And the reason why they have not got rid of him is because the majority of the blacks do not perceive him as public enemy number one—the enemy of the people—on the contrary they perceive him as citizen number one and the people's only real friend.

CHAPTER TEN

In Conclusion: No Zuma or ANC for 2013?

How's this for an unashamed white racist email from the white Afrikaner John Vorster in South Africa that was published in January 6th, 2013, in the *City Press* newspaper under the heading "No Zuma or ANC for 2013?"

"Several friends and I have decided to no longer read papers that carry articles and photographs of Zuma or the ANC. There is a better life outside there! It is a New Year's resolution we will and can keep. As South [white] Africans we have been shamed and embarrassed so often. We want to stop and smell the roses. We prefer that to the pong, deceit and lies from the empty brain cells of our current politicians. The cadre government, too, is holding the media hostage because of state advertising revenues. Have you ever considered that we are already in a dictatorship and in a far worse position than Zimbabwe? It took Mugabe just over 20 years for the chameleon to turn into a vicious and poisonous spitting cobra. What is the duty of the newspapers? Do something to bring the truth and reality to the masses and stop supporting Zuma and his henchmen. Wait for only a very short period after Madiba [Nelson Mandela] goes. He is the only man between sanity and the mother of all African explosions."

If this guy is not descended from or related to the former racist prime minister of South Africa, John Vorster, in the days of apartheid, he sounds as though he ought to be!

As for enjoying the scent of roses, in order to avoid the stench, we should remember what these roses were like in the seriously smelly days of apartheid when Prime Minister John Vorster had to resign in 1978 (to be succeeded by P. W. Botha) for his Department of Information's misuse of government funds, he who had been sent to prison during World War II in South Africa for his support of Hitler's Germany in its fascist war against Britain and the Allies.

For this act of treason—he hoped for a German victory over Britain and its allies—Vorster could have been executed by South Africa's pro-British prime minister, the aforesaid Jan Smuts, who showed some leniency and sent Vorster to jail instead; whereupon Vorster told his friends that Smuts ought to have executed him, because he never would have made the same mistake of showing such leniency himself. He would execute people for treason, he said, including Nelson Mandela (except to say that Judge de Wit had to show just a little leniency, like Jan Smuts before him, and did not execute Nelson and his colleagues for treason, but, as we have seen, gave them life imprisonment instead!).

Vorster succeeded the apostle of apartheid, Prime Minister Hendrik Verwoerd, after he had been assassinated, and it was Vorster who corruptly used his secret government slush fund to found an English-language newspaper that favored his Nationalist Party's apartheid policies. It was called *The Citizen*. Balthazar Johannes Vorster was the son of a wealthy sheep rancher in Jamestown, South Africa, and also a member of the extremely puritanical and not infrequently fanatical Dutch Reform Church. He dominated with an iron fist during the most turbulent period of apartheid with the support of the pernicious and notorious Broederbund secret society among others (one of the accused wannabe assassins of President Zuma, in chapter five of this book, is a member of the Broederbund). Balthazar Vorster was grandly named after one of the three wise men in the book of Daniel, but few today (or even back then) are rash enough to describe this appalling racist as either racially or politically wise. As for his religious and associated moral wisdom, never go there! I leave readers to judge for themselves.

Far from being politically wise, Vorster was pigheaded and ominous, but even so he had the reputation of being charming (as well as chilling!)—just as, today, President Jacob Zuma has the reputation of being charismatic.

Vorster was a law graduate of Stellenbosch University who died on September 11, 1983, at sixty-seven years of age from a blood clot in one of his lungs, having served as prime minister of apartheid South Africa from 1966 to 1978. As we know, Nelson Mandela died of a recurring lung infection this year as a result of tuberculosis that he contracted behind bars on Robben Island, far from the smell of roses (except to say that Nelson was a rare rose incarnate).

So, as we see, Vorster did not have any roses worth smelling or crowing about, given the great apartheid stench that he generated that lingers on in some white racist quarters in South Africa this day. He never had a rose garden and—I beg your pardon—he never promised the blacks one! Along with the blistering sunshine came a lot of smelly rain, not sometimes, but all the time. It is against this not too far distant background that his namesake today refers to a black African stench for which he holds President Zuma and his friends responsible, while he and his white friends prefer to smell the metaphorical roses.

What roses are these, then?

Are they pure white only, or gathered together in a refreshing multicolored bunch? It is mind-boggling how the racists among us never learn the error of their wicked ways, putting their ways out of mind and sight as history moves on and they stand still. This happens in all countries, not just South Africa of course.

But at least in the United Kingdom and other parts of Europe, racism, anti-Semitism, and color prejudice are all constantly under scrutiny and attack by and in retreat from truly rose-smelling whites who have cleaned up Britain's racial act for more than half a century now, showing other nations the way if they are interested to follow, just as the late Nelson

Mandela has shown South Africa and the world the way if it is interested to follow.

It was Prime Minister Vorster whose apartheid regime introduced house arrests, massively curtailed the freedom of movement of blacks and other coloreds, and introduced ninety-day detentions of blacks and Indians. This was when the Dutch-Afrikaner whites had the upper hand and the whip hand in South Africa. He boasted that his detentions could be extended to "this side of eternity" as he introduced his notorious police state. A police state is what white Afrikaners are falsely accusing President Zuma of right now. Vorster was completely and stupidly wrong about how long his extensions could be extended because he hadn't reckoned on the amazing qualities and global appeal of the late Nelson Mandela and all the support that he was getting in Britain and other countries of the world (in those love-hate days, the Dutch-Afrikaners in South Africa, hatefully referred to pro-ANC and pro-Mandela Brits as "nigger lovers").

No wonder President Zuma rightly believes, as he has sometimes said, that sectors of South Africa's white press are racially and politically prejudiced against him, and for *City Press* to have published such an absurd and malicious email as this—from a racist and dictatorial reader actually threatening not to read any papers that dare to mention President Zuma or carry his photographs!—does not put it in a good inter-racial light.

While the foregoing email is laughably stupid and not worth the paper it was printed on, it does reflect quite a lot of racially obnoxious and dangerous white thinking in South Africa today. Certainly, it is aimed at stirring up racist emotions against Zuma and fanning the flames of white racist thinking, given that this is neither fair comment, nor accurate or news-worthy comment, or journalism. It is, rather, pure white racist sentiment. So why publish it?

It is as if whites of this Vorster-like mentality hope and pray that the ANC train will be derailed, merely in order for them to prove that they were right about the blacks all along as they struggle to save their white faces still, some two decades after ANC rule. The all-too-obvious reason why Vorster's email is racially prejudiced and politically biased scare-mongering is that South Africa is by no stretch of the loony imagination a "dictatorship" or "in a far worse position than Zimbabwe." Such unintelligent and wildly over the top, hysterical exaggerations get the political arguments of Zuma's detractors nowhere.

It may or may not go the same way as Zimbabwe in the years ahead, but if it does, the whites will be as much to blame as anybody or everybody else, and it won't all be the fault of President Zuma. What more, exactly, is the ANC expected to do that the white and other political parties are proposing that it should do to save the intolerable situation of South Africa's millions of unemployed and grossly underpaid?

Don't all answer at once!

If today's South Africa was the black dictatorship that is alleged here, John Vorster's email would not have been published (in the absence of a free press and freedom of expression, right?), and Vorster would have been arrested and locked up for daring to send it!

And as for the masses to whom John Vorster wants the press to bring "truth and reality," they are an overwhelming 75–80 percent of black South Africans, the "truth and reality" of whom is that they much prefer, like it or not, the ANC and its latest president, as they are entitled to do in their own freedom-loving and democratic country, and why wouldn't they? Which is why they have given their support and votes, freely and democratically, to Zuma and their beloved party, which is not an apartheid party or a dictatorship like the white Afrikaner apartheid parties and governments before the ANC, and in no way comparable therefore, to President Mugabe and his government in Zimbabwe.

The City Press and its writers and editors are not infrequently rubbishing or "monstering" President Zuma, and the newspaper published a satirical "protest" poster of him last year, giving him the head of the Communist dictator of the Soviet Union, Vladimir Lenin, and large black genitals hanging outside his trousers! This was the artwork of a South African artist called Brett Murray. Its purpose was to dramatically and distastefully remind people that their allegedly womanizing black president is a polygamist with several wives who has also been charged (unsuccessfully) with rape, in addition to having allegedly had unprotected sex with a woman who was reportedly HIV-positive.

Satirizing and making sexual fun of President Zuma, with an illustrated poster of this sort, Brett Murray had an outraged ANC up in arms, as well as thousands of its supporters who protested about this protest-poster by taking to the streets with a hastily arranged protest march of their own, demanding that the mighty penis poster be removed. The masses were up in arms in defense of President Zuma while Brett Murray had gotten the whole of South Africa, Africa, and the outside world talking about Zuma's penis, because in no time at all his artwork was all over the Internet, as well as making headlines in newspapers way beyond South African shores.

While unfanatical black South Africans were too civilized to try to kill Brett Murray—they were Christians after all—they certainly wanted his poster and *The City Press* killed off, many of them, because they told people to boycott it, and no doubt advertisers had their usual second thoughts about advertising in it.

Perhaps Brett Murray should create a whole load of other posters of the sexual exploits of eminent others right across the world and fill an entire art gallery with them. We live in a sex-crazed world indeed, with all the usual hypocrisy that goes with it (where would we be without the latter, and where would Brett Murray be without it?).

Using satire to attack people with mockery in order to get them to reform their moral failings and absurdities is as old as the hills. It is all well and good as long as the principle is applied to one and all equally, and not just to some rather than others, simply because we do not like them for political or racial reasons (or simply because they are black and not white); it is all well and good as long as some are not singled out and discriminated against when others are not, merely because satirists are politically or racially prejudiced against them, rather than being genuinely morally concerned and against them and all others for having slipped below the standards of civilized behavior and moral rightness in the mind of the satirist.

Clearly, President Zuma was being singled out, stereotyped, and possibly humiliated as a big bad sexually threatening black man, but to be fair, if any of these sexual allegations against him were or are true, he still has some way to go to catch up with many of the aforementioned others. But exactly how does President Zuma compare as an alleged sexual threat or predator—or otherwise as a sexually moral letdown—to white child-abusing Catholic bishops and priests with children in their tender care, brown-skinned Indian members of Parliament, and white members of British royalty, or the former President Clinton in the United States for that matter?

The thing is, there's no end to freedom of expression, so where to draw the line between freedom of expression in a free society and the rights of individuals not to have their personal dignity or privacy unfairly and improperly abused? What is sauce for the goose is sauce for the gander, is it not? And if some behave in a sexually improper way, and then get sexually satirized for it in posters that are deliberately improper in order to make the improper point, then why not all others as well?

While a few were able to shrug off this Zuma poster in South Africa as an amusing piece of satire that had a fair or an unfair point to make—and others said that Zuma had it coming—a great many others were definitely not amused and wanted the poster removed. So they burned copies of *The City Press* on the streets, which alarmed the paper so much that it soon bowed to mass protests and removed the offending poster-facsimile from its website, fearing the worst no doubt (two members of the public had already gone into the Newman Gallery and vandalized the real poster). The ANC declared that Brett Murray's poster "violated" Zuma's "individual right to dignity," whereupon black and white female and male others responded that dignity and respect in a free country—that is a constitutional democracy—have to be earned. They said that they were not at the dictates of a president whose allegedly vulgar and undignified sexual exploits do not deserve respect.

The poster was entitled "The Spear," a sexual pun and reminder that Zuma once belonged to the military arm of the ANC that was called the Spear. In the end, the original poster in the Newman art gallery did not get sold to the visiting German couple who thought they had bought it because, having been vandalized, it had become damaged goods, and the ANC government had also declared that they would not let the poster leave the country. So the poster died, especially when the facsimile of it was withdrawn from *The City Press* website and the printed copies were destroyed (while a groveling apology was published in the newspaper for having published and promoted the poster in the first place).

So all's well that ends well. But what a mighty storm in a teacup this penis poster had caused.

On a completely different and yet not so different issue, to do with President Zuma observing that South Africa's whites spend more on their household pets than they do on their domestic black workers (as we have already heard in these pages)—gardeners and house cleaners—another reader, Tshepo Kobane, emailed *The City Press* to say: "What is wrong with President Zuma's comment? Generally speaking 'white' South Africans spend more on their dogs than they pay their 'domestics' or 'gardeners' . . . President Zuma should be commended for making such an important issue public." Indeed he should, and probably will therefore, in the next election.

Because the average white family in South Africa earns six times more than the average black, this is an issue that needs to be addressed, just as it would in any other country; not that it will be addressed by most whites if left to their own devices, or by professional Indians either, one of whom told me that "poor blacks prefer living in shantytown shacks than in proper homes, because that is what they are used to and feel comfortable with."

Given that the English-trained, world-renowned Indian human-rights lawyer Mahatma Gandhi, who spent twenty-one years in South Africa, was at least unconsciously racist against blacks in Phoenix, it is perhaps not surprising to find Indians who are as color prejudiced and racist against blacks as there are whites who are consciously color prejudiced against Indians (when they are not being prejudiced against blacks as well!).

For some of the twenty-one years that he spent in South Africa, Gandhi practiced law in Johannesburg before returning to his native India in 1914 to fight British colonial rule there. But when a bronze statue to honor Gandhi's resistance to apartheid and colonial white racism was unveiled in the City of Johannesburg in 2003 and was welcomed by Nelson Mandela, many blacks were up in arms about it. This was because they reckoned that Gandhi had shown nothing but contempt for black people by reason of written and verbal statements that he made about them, suggesting that they were lazy and could never rule themselves.

Gandhi's black critics claim that he had no love or respect for blacks and did indeed regard them as the racially inferior "untouchables" of South Africa. While he championed the cause of Indians, he stands accused of having done nothing for blacks, and according to the Johannesburg daily newspaper, *This Day*, Gandhi made a speech in Bombay in 1896 claiming that the British and other Europeans were seeking to degrade Indians to the low level of the "raw kaffir [black] whose occupation is hunting and whose sole ambition is to collect a certain number of cattle to buy a wife with, and then pass his life in indolence and nakedness." Referring to a critical book about Gandhi by the Indian author G. B. Singh, *This Day* told us that, from all the collected family and other photographs of Gandhi in South Africa, not one black face showed up, either in the vicinity where Gandhi lived or among his circle.

While, for political reasons, Gandhi identified with the liberation struggle for all nonwhites, it is claimed that he did nothing for blacks, and that he wrote and spoke only of them as obvious racial inferiors (the fact that the Indian Embassy in Pretoria has declined to comment on or object to this is interesting, is it not?). I have read Gandhi's writings, and it is certainly true that he had a racist view of blacks once upon a time, just like so many whites, Dutch-Afrikaners, and other Asians and Arabs besides (the Arabs were the first to enslave blacks). When he was forced to share a cell with blacks, Gandhi wrote that "many of the native prisoners are only one degree removed from the animal and often created rows and fought among themselves."

But one guesses that Gandhi learned the error of his racist ways in due course—as did the British and others in India and South Africa—when he became more racially enlightened later on and saw the larger picture in the fullness of time. Obviously the thing to remember about racism and color prejudice is that we have all, of course, been there and done that, and having done it, learned our lessons and hopefully repented from it. If we haven't learned our lessons and repented, then there really is no hope for any of us, and especially in a racially divided country like South Africa.

Of course, nobody can possibly know what the long-term outcome of events will be in South Africa and other parts of the world today, or even in the near future, and it is idle, not to say pretentious, to pretend that anyone can, or that it is even worth the effort trying to predict this. Life and politics are too much of a game of chance for any easy political or economic answers, and, with regard to South Africa, there are many possible scenarios on offer from pessimists and optimists alike, from extremists and ideologues, racists and multiculturalists, not to mention the usual outright prophets of doom.

And it remains to be seen whether Zuma's enemies will be able to dig up enough dirt on him behind the scenes in order to make it stick in court and bring him down before long. Certainly, his enemies are out to get him and to find allegations that can be proven against him, but thus far they have failed miserably to do so. No other ANC South African president has experienced such a concentrated effort by such an aggressive minority to get rid of him, and no other ANC president can have survived so much mudslinging and so many smear tactics. But Zuma is a survivor. All these failed allegations against him have managed to do so far is to confuse the issue and create the kind of smokescreen that makes it impossible for ordinary and not so ordinary people to know whether or not there is truth or not in any of this. If there is, maybe his political and racial enemies, with all their racial malice of forethought, will get him in due course, but if there is not, then he will go down in history for having made them look very silly, ill-advised, racially prejudiced, and pathetic indeed.

If there is a conscious or unconscious message in this book—as there often are messages beneath the surface of the written page in books, even when authors have not set out to deliberately write a message, or are even aware that they have unearthed one or been guided by one—I guess, on reflection, that it is that South Africa can and must continue to honor the legacy of Nelson Mandela and remain the brilliant brain-child of its founding father.

These are early days yet, but there is still a lot to play for, and, as we have seen in these pages, it is no secret what Mandela stood for—freedom, democracy, rule of law, sanity, decency, morality, interracial goodwill, harmony, and reconciliation in a racially divided rainbow nation. All these things and more still remain within the country's continuing grasp now that Mandela has gone, and they can continue to do so even when he is long gone, given that his legacy is truly honored, as he would certainly have wished.

All South Africa's leaders need to do is to stick to the caring Mandela rules, while at the same time, somehow urgently finding a way—being actively seen to be finding a way—of *doing much more than hitherto* for the nation's horrendously poverty-stricken millions as a top priority from here on. Many countries have had their horrendously poverty-stricken millions and not made a total mess of things—to a greater or lesser extent—and there is no reason why South Africa cannot be among them with or without Mandela, providing it remains true to itself, considering the head start that the late Nelson Mandela has given it. All countries have or have had their extreme hardships and their ups and downs, and their inequalities, economically and otherwise, but they have still remained true to themselves, as South Africa must do.

But I will stick my neck out and make one prediction—there certainly will continue to be a President Zuma and an ANC in South Africa for 2013, in answer to the question posed in the aforesaid racially offensive email from *City Press*—"No Zuma or ANC for 2013?"

On this note—and with this conclusion—I end my story.
What more is there to say?
Does one need to say?